Understanding Depression

Recent Titles in Psychology Briefs

Dealing with Anxiety
Rudy Nydegger

Suicide Prevention
Kristine Bertini

UNDERSTANDING DEPRESSION

Rudy Nydegger

Psychology Briefs

PRAEGER™

An Imprint of ABC-CLIO, LLC

Santa Barbara, California • Denver, Colorado

Library of Congress Cataloging-in-Publication Data

Names: Nydegger, Rudy V., 1943-
    Title: Understanding depression / Rudy Nydegger.
    Description: Santa Barbara, California : Praeger, [2016] | Series: Psychology briefs |
Includes bibliographical references and index.
    Identifiers: LCCN 2015039115 | ISBN 9781440842320 (hardback) | ISBN
9781440842337 (ebook)
    Subjects: LCSH: Depression, Mental. | Depression, Mental—Treatment. | BISAC:
PSYCHOLOGY / Psychopathology / Depression. | PSYCHOLOGY / Mental Illness.
    Classification: LCC RC537 .N92 2016 | DDC 616.85/27—dc23 LC record available
at http://lccn.loc.gov/2015039115

ISBN: 978-1-4408-4232-0
EISBN: 978-1-4408-4233-7

20 19 18 17   2 3 4 5

This book is also available on the World Wide Web as an eBook.
Visit www.abc-clio.com for details.

Praeger
An Imprint of ABC-CLIO, LLC

ABC-CLIO, LLC
130 Cremona Drive, P.O. Box 1911
Santa Barbara, California 93116-1911

This book is printed on acid-free paper ∞

Manufactured in the United States of America

Contents

Preface

Depression is one of the most common mental health problems affecting old and young, men and women, and people from all ethnic and cultural groups around the world. When undiagnosed and/or untreated, this specific problem results in significant expenses for patients, their families, the health care system, and for society as well; appropriate therapy for this very treatable disorder costs only a fraction of all of the other expenses for this condition. We know that over 80 percent of those who suffer from depression will improve when treated, but less than 20 percent of depressed people will actually receive appropriate treatment.

This book explores depression, the differing types of depressive disorders, and the differences between "clinical" and "normal" depression and how it can be treated. Since depression affects people in various ways, it is important to understand how each society and culture responds to depression relative to gender, age, ethnicity, race, sexual orientation, as well as other variables. The book also examines the many different types of psychological and medical forms of treatment for depression and their effectiveness and limitations. In addition to current treatments we will also explore some of the newer and experimental forms of treatment and how they may be of value in the future. Further, many alternative treatments are discussed, and the research evidence for their value is also examined.

Although this book relies upon the most current and valid research, the material offered here is presented in language that is accessible to a broad general audience. When technical terms are used, they are accompanied by definitions and explanations. The reader can be sure that they are reading the best and most recent professional information, but in a manner that is understandable and clear. In addition, the book's author, Dr. Rudy Nydegger, has been a practicing clinical psychologist, a professor of psychology, a researcher, and an author for over forty years. The goal of this book is to present the reader with the necessary information to develop a better understanding and appreciation for depression and the issues associated with this disorder.

1

What Is Depression?

INTRODUCTION

Depression is an equal opportunity disorder. It can affect anyone of any group, background, race, gender, age—anyone. It is the great leveler and can reduce the greatest and the smallest of us to the pain and nothingness that is depression.

Depression profoundly impacts the lives and health of millions of people around the world. Of course, all of us have, from time to time, experienced "mood swings" and may believe that we have experienced clinical depression, or that we at least understand what it feels like. Experiencing a difficult or traumatic event, a significant disappointment, the death of someone close, or a failed relationship can lead to emotional reactions that certainly feel like depression. Depression, however, is more than experiencing a difficult day or event or a miserable mood. For example, depressed mood is not the same as a depressive disorder. Depressed mood refers to a negative affective or emotional quality such as feeling sadness, unhappiness, etc., for an unspecified time period. A depressive disorder refers to a list of possible symptoms that must be considered prior to making a diagnosis, and the symptoms must exist for a specific period of time.

From a treatment point of view the professional must know precisely what led the person to seek help and what conditions preceded this decision. Having a complete and accurate picture of the disorder and the symptoms will lead to a proper diagnosis that will help to understand and treat the patient. When we say "clinical disorder," this means that the presenting depressive symptoms satisfy the conditions of a depressive disorder to warrant an official diagnosis.

Interestingly, many think of depression as a singular disorder when in fact there are several types of depression as well as other types of disorders that include negative moods. Additionally, depression will often accompany other medical or psychological conditions, clouding the diagnosis and complicating treatment planning even further. Those who suffer from depression will often experience emotional, motivational, behavioral, cognitive, and physical symptoms. Emotionally, for example, patients may feel miserable, empty, sad, humiliated, and worthless. From a motivational point of view patients may lack the desire to do much of anything, including a decreased interest in work or school, social activities, or any of those things that used to be enjoyable to them. Behaviorally, depressed people show decreased activity levels, often isolate from others, and stay in bed far longer than they need for normal sleep and rest; they also do not have much energy or desire to get involved in anything that requires effort or attention. We also see different types of thinking patterns in depressed people, for example, a negative view of self, their situation, and future, and pessimistic thoughts about almost everything. Depressed persons often report that they are not functioning well intellectually and frequently have problems with short-term memory, attention, and concentration. Finally, people who suffer from depression often complain of a number of physical symptoms that are sometimes rather vague and diffuse, such as headaches, indigestion, constipation, dizzy spells, general pain, and sexual dysfunction.

SYMPTOMS OF DEPRESSION

Officially, the American Psychiatric Association's *Diagnostic and Statistical Manual* contains a specific set of symptoms that are used to diagnose the different types of depression, and these will be discussed in more detail in a later chapter. The two basic core characteristics of depression are depressed mood and a lack of interest or enjoyment in things formerly found to be enjoyable. In addition, depressed persons usually report having sleep difficulties including falling asleep or staying asleep (*insomnia*), or oversleeping but still never feeling that they get enough sleep (*hypersomnia*).

Other physical symptoms of depression include extremes in nutrition and activity levels. Some depressed people cannot eat and have no appetite, resulting in weight loss. Others seem to "feed" depression, often with poor nutritional choices like sugars and other simple carbohydrates.

In this case overeating, poor food choices, and a lack of activity usually lead to weight gain. In addition, the poor food choices may also create other nutritional problems that may complicate the patient's medical situation. For example, blood sugar problems like hypoglycemia (low blood sugar) or high blood pressure (from too much salt or other factors) can be the result of poor food choices.

Most depressed people experience reduced energy and lower activity levels; however, occasionally some appear anxious or agitated. In addition, negative feelings about themselves and a general pessimism can be found in any type of depression. The depressed person finds it difficult to think positively about him- or herself or anything else and may think often about death or suicide. Most patients explain that they do not want to die, but rather that they cannot see a compelling reason to continue living, and that doing anything to end the pain and suffering of depression would be a welcome respite. It is also common for depressed people to describe a lack of cognitive and intellectual efficiency and to feel that they are not thinking clearly.

Major depression is frequently misdiagnosed or missed entirely and is often untreated for long periods of time. One reason is that the symptoms can be indicative of other types of problems; another reason is that many will not seek help due to the possible stigma or due to the belief that nothing will help. Many depressed people are so fatigued and discouraged that they cannot force themselves even go to an appointment. Others don't know that they are depressed because it is how they feel most of the time, and it may seem almost "normal" to them; they may not even be aware of the fact that they are actually experiencing symptoms of depression.

IMPAIRMENT ASSOCIATED WITH DEPRESSION

To diagnose depression we look for symptoms that interfere with a person's ability to function and for signs that the patient is not experiencing a "normal" emotional state. The symptoms of depression are subjectively experienced as unpleasant or dysfunctional and are "abnormal" relative to one's own normal emotional state.

Depressed people usually report low self-esteem and are very critical of themselves and discouraged about almost everything. They often believe that they don't *deserve* to feel good and that being depressed is a punishment for being so worthless. Understandably, if one is feeling negative about oneself it is unlikely that the depressed person will show a high level of mastery in their jobs, their relationships, and other activities, which results in feeling even more discouraged. One of the most difficult aspects of depression is that the feeling of worthlessness can lead to eventually just giving up. In fact, depressed persons feel so fatigued and tired of performing poorly that they may choose not do anything at all rather than to keep failing. More precisely, depressed people will usually perceive themselves as failing even if those around them do not agree. When this downward spiral begins it is difficult to stop, and before long others will recognize the performance and behavioral problems.

THE COSTS OF DEPRESSION

During any one year period about 9.5 percent of the population in the United States, or about 20.9 million adults, suffer from some type of depression, and we are not sure how many cases go undetected. According to some, major depressive disorder (MDD) is the leading cause of disability in the United States. They point out that MDD results in more days of disability, lost work days, and presenteeism (when a person shows up to work too sick, impaired, stressed out, or distracted to be productive) than many other medical conditions, creating a huge financial burden for employers. The cost of lost work hours, medical expenses, reduced effectiveness, and other related problems due to depression affect every one of us. Not only are employers impacted but so are other employees, customers, insurance carriers, family members, and friends. Various estimates of the direct and indirect costs of depression on well-being and national prosperity in the United States is in excess of $80 billion per year; since this data is over 10 years old it is likely that this number is much higher now.

It is difficult to determine the extent to which other people, in addition to the depressed patient, are actually impacted by the disorder. It has been claimed that depression is associated with excess disability, impaired health, lower quality of life, and lower well-being for patients *and* their significant others. Depression may be the most serious emotional problem among disabled persons, which suggests that of all of the disabling conditions the total impact of depression may actually exceed any other medical or psychological disability. The true cost of depression must also include the effect it has on the lives, jobs, relationships, etc. of those living around the depressed patient; depression is clearly one of the most pressing public health issues in the United States today.

One factor that is often overlooked by health and mental health professionals is the impact of depression upon other psychological and medical conditions. Physicians and other health professionals do not always recognize depression as a major health risk. One set of studies followed depressed men and women for several years in order to determine how their health status was affected by depression. They found that, after controlling for other conditions, people with minor depression were more likely to die of another condition in succeeding years than people who were not depressed; this was particularly true of men.

MISSING THE DIAGNOSIS OF DEPRESSION

Symptoms of depression are so unpleasant and intrusive in one's work, relationships, pleasurable activities, and most other aspects of life that it may seem odd that depression could be frequently missed or misdiagnosed. Even if the depressed person does not want to seek help, family and friends can encourage them to see a professional to discuss the many effective treatments that are available today.

Why would a person who feels so miserable resist getting help? We know that many people, and especially men, are reluctant to pursue professional treatment because of the stigma or because it seems "weak" to seek help for something as "simple" as depression. Tragically, many people are reluctant to seek treatment because they are embarrassed and fear the reaction of people they know. Still others have no knowledge at all about the symptoms of depression and assume that their feelings are "normal" and certainly do not require professional help.

Many people are not aware of the fact that help is available and that you do not need to consider yourself "crazy" in order to qualify for professional help. It is a good idea to begin by seeing a primary care physician (PCP) who can rule out other physical conditions that have similar symptoms to depression. The first line of treatment for depression is often medication, which can be prescribed by a PCP rather than a psychiatrist or psychopharmacologist. However, if a person is *only* receiving medication from a non–mental health professional and is not receiving therapy from anyone else, the patient is not likely to be receiving adequate treatment. A PCP is qualified to prescribe psychotropic medications (drugs for psychiatric conditions), as it is sometimes difficult in some areas to find a psychiatrist who can see a new patient without a considerable wait. Although some treatment is better than none, we will discuss in later chapters how treatment must involve coordinated psychological and medical approaches for optimal effectiveness.

Depression is frequently misdiagnosed or missed altogether by health professionals and can easily be confused with other conditions. Another unfortunate reality of medical care today is that physicians are under pressure to see as many patients as possible and often do not have the time to listen carefully to detect the subtle indicators of depression. Some of the aches and pains that a patient presents may actually be related to depression, but in the absence of other indicators the physician simply may not "see" the depression. In addition, many people believe that all depression is a temporary condition and that if you just leave it alone it will disappear by itself. Fatigue and lack of motivation are common symptoms of depression that often put the patient in the difficult position of not wanting or being able to do those things that may help them.

Finally, and tragically, many people do not receive the treatment that they need for depression and for many other conditions because they simply do not have access to services. They may lack insurance or the ability to pay for services, lack transportation to get to appointments, or mental health services may not be available in their community. Society is making choices about health care, and specifically mental health care, that are preventing millions of people from receiving the help they deserve. This may seem a harsh statement, but the evidence clearly points to this conclusion.

SUICIDE

The most tragic result of depression is suicide—when a person feels so helpless and hopeless that he or she would rather die than continue feeling as they do. Depression, especially major depression, and bipolar disorder (another type of mood disorder) have significant risk factors for suicide. There is rarely one specific reason for attempting or committing suicide, and survivors often say that they do not necessarily want to die but want to end the pain. However, if a person is at risk for suicide the motive or reasons are irrelevant—regardless of "why" they may want to end their life, we need to figure out *now* what needs to be done to keep them safe. Comments such as "He/She is just trying to get attention" or "It wasn't a serious attempt, so don't worry about it" are not very helpful. It is important to stabilize the situation, keep the person safe, and then determine what type of treatment intervention can be immediately utilized.

Studies indicate that suicide is the eleventh leading cause of death among all ages in the United States. Recent statistics report that about 30,000 people commit suicide in the United States each year and that 730,000 persons who attempt suicide each year do not successfully complete the act. In fact, successful suicides outnumber homicides in the United States by 3 to 2, and over 90 percent of people who die by suicide suffer from either depression or some other mental or substance use disorder.

Some facts about suicide:

- Suicide is a major complication of depression.
- 1 in 16 people with major depression die by suicide.
- About 2/3 of people who die by suicide are depressed.
- Highest risk factors:
  - older white males
  - people who live alone
  - people who have had prior suicide attempts
  - those who refuse psychiatric/psychological evaluation
  - people who abuse alcohol and/or drugs
- Women attempt suicide 3–4 times more often than men.
- Men are 3–4 times more likely to commit suicide than women.
- The risks are particularly high in people with bipolar disorder—about 25–50 percent of patients with bipolar disorder attempt suicide at least once.

One study found that those with a serious physical illness were more than six times more likely to commit suicide. Someone who is experiencing a lingering and painful illness may be more likely to commit suicide to escape from significant pain, increasing disability, being a burden to others, etc. However, the fact that suicide might make sense to a suffering patient does not mean that we should abandon our efforts to provide the most meaningful treatment for any person suffering from a serious depressive episode.

Suicide is also significant among adolescents and young adults and is the third leading cause of death between the ages of 15–24. Evidence reports that depression and suicide have increased substantially in both men and women over the past century. Presently, we find that the suicide rate is lowest in the 5–14 age group, then increases dramatically in the 15–24 age group, and finally remains fairly level at about 16/100,000 persons until the 65–74 age group where it begins to increase through the mid-80s. Other interesting findings relate suicide to marital status. Out of 100,000 persons in the United States, 12.4 married people, 18.4 single people, 21.8 widowed persons, and 37.3 divorced persons commit suicide; clearly, divorce can be an important risk factor for suicide. There is no single reason why someone chooses to end their life. While each case is unique, observed patterns shed light on some of the different motives people consider before attempting suicide.

- Death seekers: These people intend to end their lives, although they will usually wax and wane in this intention. From a prevention perspective it is a very difficult situation because this person can shift their intention from minute to minute. However, clinicians will help a person to develop coping skills to deal with the dangerous periods when they are at higher risk. The patient will hopefully continue treatment to keep them safe.

- Death initiators: These people also want to end their lives, but they have very different reasons. They act upon the idea that their death is a virtual certainty in the near future, and they are simply hurrying the process. It is thought that the author Ernest Hemmingway was in this category. One of the main reasons he committed suicide was that he felt his body and his health were failing him; his death was simply a matter of time. Rather than watch himself slide into ill health and incapacity, he sped up the process that was already in place.

- Death ignorers: This is a very interesting and troubling pattern. People in this group actively and intentionally kill themselves. However, they do not believe that this act will end their existence; rather, it will help them move to another even better level of existence. This pattern is often found among cult members who participate in mass suicide or among suicide bombers who feel that their act will send them straight to heaven. If they are correct, of course, then the act is not self-destructive but rather self-actualizing. If they are wrong, then the act is a delusional self-deception with a tragic and unnecessary outcome.

- Death darers: These people seem to have ambivalent feelings about death and engage in very risky behaviors that could possibly end their lives. The behavior is intentional but the outcome is uncertain. Often, when queried, these people say that risking death makes them feel even more alive. When questioned further about how they feel about the prospect of dying as a result of this behavior, they usually say something like, "Then it was meant to be," or "That is the way I would like to go." A good example is a person who plays "Russian Roulette"; they could easily die from the act but they might survive it as well.

In addition to these patterns of "intentional" suicide, there is another pattern that is referred to as "subintentional death." In this type of situation the person has an indirect, covert, partial, or subconscious role in their own suicide. Thus, their behavior may lead to their death, but the intention is not obvious. In cases where the person survives the attempt, they might even deny the intentionality. For example, a person who is terminally ill and who doesn't really intend to kill himself makes a mistake with the medication and "accidentally" overdoses, which leads to death. In reality we might never know for sure if the person intended to commit suicide, but we must keep in mind that there are cases when the intention is not clear even if the outcome is.

A similar pattern was mentioned by Menninger, who described what he called "chronic suicide." This pattern refers to people who behave in life-endangering ways over extended periods of time, knowing that it will probably result in death. Since their death will occur in the future, they will often say something like, "Well, you can't live forever," or some such platitude. The behaviors Menninger is referring to are patterns such as smoking, drug or alcohol abuse, very risky occupations, or any form of consistent behavior that will likely result in death—eventually, at least.

In order to understand the reasons and dynamics of suicide, many researchers and clinicians have recently focused on the cognitive aspects of suicide—that is, how a person's thoughts and perceptions are related to the attempt or commission of suicide. For example, it is frequently noted that most people who are suicidal feel helpless and hopeless. They think that things are unbearable and nothing they do will change that (helpless), and that it will continue or worsen in the future and nothing they can do will prevent it (hopeless). It has been demonstrated that feeling helpless and hopeless is a better predictor of suicide than just the diagnosis of depression. Deficits in problem-solving skills and especially in social and interpersonal problem solving are also cognitive issues that are related to suicide. Clearly, what researchers and clinicians are telling us is that at some level the way people think, and not just their emotions, significantly contribute to the decision to attempt suicide.

It is important to learn about the many warning signs that indicate that a person is contemplating suicide. Most persons who end their lives were somewhat ambivalent about the act; for example, many people will visit their PCP when feeling depressed and suicidal but will not mention those feelings so the physician does not detect the problem. This potential situation does not question the competence of the PCP but rather stresses that at some level patients who are looking for assistance do not reveal to their doctors their feelings of hopelessness and helplessness. It is important, therefore, that all of us be aware of the typical warning signs of depression and suicidality and be prepared to take appropriate action. Some of the warning signs we can look for include:

- Social isolation (usually self-imposed)
- Drastic mood swings or personality changes

- Neglecting their home, financial responsibilities, or pets
- Recent psychological trauma
- Exaggerated complaints of aches and pains
- Giving away special possessions
- "Putting things in order"
- Sudden calm or even cheerfulness after a period of depression
- Frequent use of alcohol or drugs
- Buying a gun
- Verbal threats of suicide or desire to die
- Family history of suicide or previous attempts

While being aware of these warning signs, it is important to keep them in perspective. Worrying about someone to the point of following and watching them constantly, calling 911 for the most minimal warning signs, etc., will not likely help and may worsen the situation. The best course of action is to talk to the person and offer to help, but not to play the role of a treating professional. Even if the person says they won't talk to a stranger, a family member or a friend cannot replace the need for a professional who has experience in dealing with suicide. A relative or a friend can offer to help find a professional and to accompany them to the appointment—their personal physician is a good place to start. Do not ever allow yourself to be put in the position of keeping someone alive. First, if they really want to kill themselves they will likely find a way to do it regardless of what you do. Second, trying to play the role of the "rescuer" will distort and disrupt the relationship that you do have with them, and third, you will be taking away from them something that they really do need—a friend. If a situation is acute and life threatening you must take emergency action—call 911, then their doctor or a relative. They may initially feel that you have betrayed them by "telling on them." That is when you need to make it clear that if you are going to make a mistake you are going to err on the side of keeping them safe.

There are few things in life more tragic, and that may appear to be senseless, than suicide. At times a suicide may seem entirely understandable and rational (e.g., someone who is dying from a painful and lingering illness), but more often than not a suicide seems like the last desperate act of someone who feels that they have no alternative. The responsibility of a treating professional is to help the suicidal patient discover some different and healthier alternatives and then to act on them. Clearly, the act of committing suicide eliminates any options that may have been available and that could have helped.

SUMMARY

The signs and symptoms of depression vary between clinically relevant depression and normal variations in mood. The functional impairments associated with depression may or may not be noticed by friends, family, and professionals, and the absence of an accurate diagnosis can delay, disrupt, or negate treatment that could help.

The costs of depression are extraordinarily high for patients, families, employers, and society at large. Worldwide, depression is a major public health and societal issue that includes enormous direct and indirect costs, but one of the biggest costs is the loss of a life due to suicide. Knowing the warning signs of depression and how best to aid someone who may be contemplating suicide are keys to assisting those in need.

2

Who Can Develop Depression and What Causes It?

INTRODUCTION

Nearly 19 million Americans suffer from depression—affecting approximately 12 percent of American women (more than 12 million persons) and 7 percent of American men (more than 6 million persons). Over the course of a whole lifetime about 21 percent of all women and 12 percent of all men will suffer from clinical depression. This leads to significant costs for victims of depression, their families, friends, work colleagues, organizations in which they work, and even society as a whole.

These statistics are impressive given the number of people who are impacted by mood disorders in general and depression specifically. In addition to the obvious harm these disorders cause in a person's life, there are many other indirect costs. For example, persons with depression use our health care systems at a higher rate than the general public, which includes an increased use of medications, more frequent emergency room visits, and more office visits to their medical providers. Since most people with depression are not appropriately diagnosed and treated, and thus cannot be counted, the true costs of depression are far higher than the studies report. Depression impacts many people both personally and professionally, and it dramatically reduces the quality and quantity of people's productivity, often ruining people's careers or seriously disrupting their educations.

GENDER, AGE, AND DEPRESSION

Historically, it has been reported that mood disorders usually emerge between the ages of 20 and 30, but they can occur at any age. Interestingly, recent research evidence shows that depression occurs earlier in life than in past decades. It is not clear whether people are developing depression earlier in life or perhaps detection is improving—most likely it is a little of both. It is true that women are diagnosed and treated for depression more frequently than men, and the reasons for this are complicated and will be discussed later in the book. Also, the elderly and nonwhite patients are much less likely to be treated for depression, and it is not because they rarely suffer from depression. The reasons for this lack of treatment will also be discussed later in this book, but the unfortunate fact remains that in all groups people with depression can be helped with appropriate treatment, and when people are not able or willing to access treatment, this is very troubling.

Although many used to feel that children rarely develop depression, we now know that children and adolescents are frequently treated for this condition. Events during childhood can contribute to an increased susceptibility to depression in adulthood, and especially traumas that involve parental abuse, substance abuse, and/or other mental health problems. Fortunately, children and adolescents with depression are being diagnosed and treated more frequently than in the past, but it is still true that most depressed youngsters do not receive adequate treatment.

SOCIAL CLASS AND DEPRESSION

Cultural and subcultural factors also influence who is more likely to develop depression, and social status is a risk factor for depression, but as one would expect, it is not a simple relationship. Several studies have shown that people in lower socioeconomic classes are more likely to suffer from depression, but the findings demonstrate only minimal differences, and it is not clear how meaningful these differences really are. Measures such as education and income do have a direct impact on depression, but the actual impact of social class on depression independent of these other factors is not clear.

Within any given social class, education is the strongest predictor of depression in women (the more educated a woman is the less likely she is to be depressed), and this is more of a risk factor than social class itself. Family income is the best predictor for men (the higher the family income, the less likely a man is to be depressed); note that this is family income rather than personal income. So, while social class is a relevant predictor of depression for both men and women, specific components of social class (education for women and family income for men) are the best single predictors of depression for those two groups. Other studies show that people with a higher income are less likely to be depressed than people of lower income since they experience fewer survival stressors and have better access to appropriate care. This does not mean that wealthier people do not get depressed, but they are less likely than people of lower income.

DEPRESSION AROUND THE WORLD

People suffer from depression in all cultures and countries. In 1990 major depressive disorder was ranked fourth in the world as a cause of disease burden following respiratory infections, diarrheal diseases, and perinatal diseases. In 2020 depression is projected to become second in disease burden in the world behind heart disease; as Third World countries get better medical care and more effective public health programs, the frequency of infectious diseases will decrease slightly, which is why heart disease and depression will likely move up higher on the list. "Disease burden" refers to the negative impact of a particular disease. This refers to financial, personal, family, social, and medical costs, and any other "burdens" imposed by a particular disease. It is very concerning to realize that a highly treatable condition like depression has such a powerful and negative impact all over the world.

Worldwide rates of depression indicate that women have a greater frequency of depression, and in the United States the rate is about twice as often as men. There are a few societies, however, where men suffer depression more frequently than women. This is an important finding because if depression were simply a biological issue the rates would be similar all over the world, but they are not.

When looking at some of the secondary and indirect effects of depression, it becomes obvious that this disorder places enormous burdens upon the families of depressed patients as well as their caregivers. Since we know that heightened stress increases the susceptibility to depression and other psychological disorders, this is particularly a serious issue for women. Women are more likely to be the caregivers for mentally or physically ill family members, and in many parts of the world they often have less access than men to health and mental health resources. This means that women will experience a disproportionate amount of the stress from caring for a depressed person, and in some countries they also might have less access to health and mental health treatment than men. Sadly, caring for a depressed person increases the risk of depression for the caregiver, which also significantly amplifies the burden on the caregiver but also on the patient and other family members.

Violence is also one of the key factors that contributes to people developing disorders such as depression, and this is obviously relative to the location and culture where they live. People victimized by violence are more susceptible to depression and are more likely to attempt and commit suicide than the general population. Since these factors depend in part on the culture in which one lives, one would expect more negative mental health problems, including depression, in cultures where violence is more common. Unfortunately, in most cultures women are more likely to be victimized by domestic violence, which places them at higher risk for depression than men.

There are certainly other factors besides violence and domestic violence that can lead to depression; being denied educational and occupational opportunities are factors that also negatively impact one's mental health, and again these outcomes are more likely to affect women than men in most cultures. The link between disorders like depression and economic deprivation can result from unemployment, being in debt, or belonging to a lower socioeconomic class in society. Once again, this particular burden disproportionately affects women, and this is true all over the world.

CAUSAL FACTORS IN DEPRESSION

When addressing the many possible causes of depression we must begin with an appreciation for the breadth of this topic, including psychological, environmental, and biological factors. Psychological factors that have been linked to depression include such things as

- Unresolved issues from childhood or early life that are manifested later
- A history of depression
- Damage to the body (injury, illness, surgery, etc.)
- Fear of death
- Frustration with bodily/psychological changes like memory
- Difficulties with coping with stress and change
- Substance abuse
- Low self-esteem
- Extreme dependency
- Chronic pessimism

Environmental factors that are related to depression include

- Loneliness/isolation
- Retirement
- Being unmarried (especially if widowed)
- Recently bereaved
- Lack of a good support system
- Decreased mobility/independence

Biological/physical factors that are related to depression include

- Genetics (inherited predisposition to depression)
- Co-morbidities (other physical or psychological conditions)
- Vascular changes in the brain
- Vitamin B-12 deficiency (there is some question as to whether this is a cause or an effect)
- Vitamin D3 deficiency
- Chronic, severe pain
- Drugs and certain medications

The National Institute of Mental Health mentions that certain illnesses (stroke, heart attack, cancer, Parkinson's, hormonal disorders) as well as other physical factors can lead to depression. They also suggest that a serious loss, relationship problems, financial difficulties, and major life changes are frequently related to the development of depression, supporting the theory that depression is usually the result of a combination of many factors and not just one or two.

BIOLOGICAL FACTORS

There are a number of different approaches that try to uncover the biological basis for depression—e.g., various glands, certain pathways in the brain—and much of the research has focused on the chemical "messengers" in the brain called neurotransmitters. With improvements in brain imaging techniques, other researchers have looked for structural changes in the brain as well as examining how the brain functions. Some forms of depression are more likely to have biological causes than others, and one single biological model will never suffice to explain everything about depression.

Some researchers are convinced that there is a biological connection between some illnesses and depression and that it is not just because an ill person is feeling depressed because they are sick. For example, nervous system conditions such as multiple sclerosis, stroke, vascular brain changes, different types of dementia, brain trauma, and others are frequently associated with depression. Other conditions like hypothyroidism, fibromyalgia, and chronic fatigue syndrome are also often associated with depression.

Drugs of all kinds can also lead to depressive symptoms. Prescription drugs and recreational or "street" drugs can precipitate a depressive episode, as can some central nervous system depressants such as alcohol, marijuana, and "downer drugs" like barbiturates, narcotics, tranquilizers, pain pills, and antipsychotic medications. Some people who are either addicted or dependent upon these drugs will buy them "on the street" to use them recreationally even if they are prescribed by their physician. Interestingly, the "energizing" drugs like amphetamines, cocaine, phencyclidine (angel dust), and others can also lead to depression but through a different pathway. Historically, some of these "energizing" types of drugs like dextroamphetamine were used to treat depression. It was thought that they could help someone who was lethargic and lacked energy due to depression. Often the result was a patient who was still depressed but was now in a state called "agitated depression." When this type of drug begins to wear off, one of the withdrawal symptoms can be a depressive state, and in a person who is high risk for depression the withdrawal from this type of drug can lead to a serious depressive reaction.

Some researchers and theorists have postulated that hormones can be related to depression. One study explores the hormonal impact and the relationship between gonadal functioning (the sex glands: testicles for men and ovaries for women) and depression. Testosterone gel may produce antidepressant effects in males with low testosterone levels who are experiencing depression. However, this finding is not always consistent, and there are probably other factors involved as well. Although there are mixed findings regarding the relationship between sex hormones (like testosterone) and depression, there is enough evidence to conclude that in some people there seems to be a relationship between these hormone levels and depression.

Frequently, depressed people report problems sleeping. Their sleep schedule, appetite, and other aspects of their life just seem to be dysregulated— that is, the normal bodily rhythms seem to be "out of whack." Some people even have a "reversed" sleep pattern where they seem to want to stay awake when others are sleeping and to sleep when others are awake. Depressed individuals never seem to have their sleep regulated in a way that is consistent with other people, or with the way they were prior to being depressed. Many depressed people enter into REM sleep (rapid eye movement sleep, during which most dreams occur) sooner than nondepressed people and experience more REM cycles during the night. This also means that they do not spend as much time in the deepest levels of sleep.

The area of biological inquiry that has stimulated the most recent interest is the study of the relationship between neurotransmitters and depression. Neurotransmitters are the chemical messengers that send information from one nerve cell to another, several of which appear to be related to depression but in a complicated way. For example, the imbalance in these chemicals can lead to depression, but we also know that when depression develops for other reasons, a chemical imbalance can be the result. Regardless of which comes first, the imbalance or the depression, the antidepressant medications work to try to re-establish normal levels of these brain chemicals in the depressed person—they may not "cure" depression, but they can frequently be helpful.

GENETICS

Another area in the biological realm of depression is the field of genetics and the types of characteristics that people inherit from their parents—such as eye and hair color, height, etc. It is common knowledge that depression tends to run in families, but there has been considerable debate as to whether this is due to heredity or to environmental influences; today the conclusion is that both have a role in depression. Even if genetics is not always the main factor causing depression, it is clear that it has some role in its development.

SOCIAL, FAMILY, AND ENVIRONMENTAL FACTORS

In addition to genetics, depression has been linked to a number of social and family processes. Some studies find that the best predictor of future depression is if depressive symptoms occur while experiencing stressful events. Others report that married people are more susceptible to depression than those who have never married, although unsupported single mothers are more likely to become depressed than others. Depression rates are also higher among divorced and widowed persons—especially men. People caring for ill or disabled patients are also at risk for depression. Caregivers are more likely to succumb to many disorders, including depression, and are more likely to die from serious diseases like cardiovascular disease, diabetes, and cancer. For caregivers and others, social isolation, financial strain, worry, and being cut off from rewarding activities can often lead to depression.

Social and environmental factors such as financial strain and decreased feelings of control and self-worth often lead to symptoms of depression. Decreased satisfaction with social contact, lower levels of perceived social support, and more disruptions in social relationships lead to depression as well. Interestingly, many studies point out that Americans today spend less time visiting family and friends, and in community service and related activities, than in the past. Today's children are more likely to come from families of divorce and are less likely to live near extended family. Materialism is more important to children and adolescents today, and students entering college now rate "living well" as more important than "developing a meaningful life philosophy," the opposite of what was found thirty years ago. Contrast these findings with research that demonstrates lower rates of depression in cultures that place high value on the home-making role and tend to be more family centered. It is possible that the "protective effect" of a supportive family/social system is not as prevalent in today's culture (at least in the United States) and may be related to higher rates of depression.

Depression, like other mental disorders, is inversely related to social class; that is, the lower the social class the greater the chance of developing many diseases—including depression. People within the lower social strata tend to deal with more stressful and difficult situations than those in more advantaged levels of society. As a result, many have concluded that depression is primarily situational; some feel that depression is more about life circumstances than genetics or other biological factors. Regardless of gender, people with more accumulated wealth tend to experience depression less frequently. When a person is at high risk for depression, their access to meaningful social support and financial security often helps to ease and even perhaps prevent its onset.

PSYCHOLOGICAL FACTORS

The oldest of the psychological approaches to understanding depression is psychoanalysis as originally developed by Sigmund Freud. This approach looks for the source of a person's difficulties in their subconscious and expects that problems in this area of psychic functioning can lead to a pathological condition like depression. Psychoanalysts tend to search for the source of an adult's difficulties in the person's history and childhood since they believe that a person develops through life's stages and will encounter certain events (trauma, for example) that can disrupt development and lead to later problems. Psychoanalytic psychotherapy is used to correct the deviations in development that were the foundation of problems, including depression.

Freud wrote about melancholia, which is similar to what we today call depression. He was not the first to write about this condition, and in fact there are references to depression or melancholia throughout recorded history. However, Freud was the first modern writer to address depression from a purely psychological perspective. Freud and one of his followers, Karl Abraham, wrote extensively on melancholia, and were among the first of the psychological theorists to systematically address depression. They both recognized the similarities between depression and grief, which led them to believe that depression is a response to loss. They also believed that the loss could be real or symbolic but that either could lay the groundwork for depression.

Several newer psychodynamic approaches to depression rely on intrapsychic factors (inside the person's mind) and developmental problems. However, the more modern theories address issues other than unconscious instincts and conflicts and look more at the conscious process and daily events.

A recent psychological approach to understanding depression is the cognitive theories that demonstrate good explanatory power, research support, and the significance of their role in the development of effective and well-supported treatment approaches. The main idea in the cognitive theories is that depression is a function at least in part of how people think. Even though depression is a disorder of mood, it may be caused or complicated by how people think about and perceive things. Cognitive theorists believe there are two types of thinking that lead to depression. Some people have developed *maladaptive attitudes* that can lead to depression. For example, people who think they are only worthwhile if everyone loves them have set themselves up to experience stress, disappointment, rejection, and ultimately depression. Depressed persons can also exhibit *errors in thinking* that may become problematic when they perceive themselves as responsible for something unfortunate they have experienced, (e.g., being diagnosed with a disease) even when they couldn't have possibly caused the event. Continuing to blame oneself in spite of others' efforts to convince them otherwise is an error in thinking that can lead to depression.

Some theorists refer to the "cognitive triad," three ways of thinking that are commonly found in depressed people:

- Negative feelings about their experiences
- Negative feelings about themselves
- Negative feelings about the future

Unlike the psychodynamic approaches that delve into the person's history and development to find the roots of depression, the cognitive approach is more direct; it addresses how the person is thinking now, how that is related to depression, and how the person can be helped to think differently.

For some patients, the relationship between how they think and how they feel is not simple, and learning to think differently may not be the only way to treat an emotional disorder such as depression. Cognition acts as a mediator between events in our lives and our moods. In other words, things happen to us, and we must find ways to think about and understand them. Some of these thinking patterns may lead to the development of different emotional states, including depression. The cognitive approach has clearly changed the way professionals think about depression and the ways we treat it as well.

Another psychological approach to depression that has been used for many decades is the behavioral approach. This approach explains that depression is a reaction to the events that people experience, and, therefore, the environment is an important part of understanding the cause and the treatment of depression. A simple explanation is that depression is due to changes in the rewards and the punishments that people receive, which leads them to perform fewer constructive acts, and therefore receive fewer rewards. This cycle continues until people receive very few rewards or positive outcomes at all, and the absence of social rewards is a very important part of depression. Conversely, if a person receives significant punishments, this will also lead to depression. It is easy to believe that the more positive experiences in one's life, the more positive feelings will result. Some behavioral theorists recognize the importance of reinforcements, but they also look at it from a cognitive perspective. They believe that when people feel they no longer have control over their rewards or punishments, they are more likely to feel helpless and develop problems, possibly leading to depression.

Some behavioral theorists also focus on the relationship between environmental influences such as stress and its impact on depression. They point out that dysthymia (a milder form of depression) may be caused by severe stress; however, they do not adequately explain why there are individual differences—that is, if several people are exposed to the same stress, why do only some of them become depressed?

The behavioral approach has been helpful in understanding the relationship between environmental events and depression and in the development of many of our treatment approaches. However, many professionals feel this approach is somewhat limited by itself. Today a major trend in the study and treatment of depression has been the merging of the cognitive and behavioral approaches. This influential model is called, appropriately enough, the cognitive-behavioral model, and is well supported in the research literature.

AN INTEGRATIVE APPROACH

The complexity of depression is due to the many factors involved in the understanding of mood disorders in general. Although all of the approaches discussed above offer some ideas to help us understand depression, how they all fit together is not so obvious. Rather than performing a microscopic analysis of each of these many factors, a more general and conceptual model is discussed next, which will help demonstrate how all of these different factors fit together.

People who are biologically predisposed to depression and/or who have suffered abuse or trauma during their early development can become more vulnerable to depression due to their current situation—such as having poor social support or no close relationships, having significant conflicts in life, or being un- or underemployed. Additional traumatic or stressful life events—including the death of a loved one, various losses and separations, as well as defeats, conflicts, and feelings of being trapped—may also contribute to depression.

Stress can lead more directly to depressive symptoms, including some physical changes that can occur in response to stressful situations. Under stress the body produces hormones that will change physical and emotional functioning and also alter the functioning of the chemical transmitter systems in the brain. Further, stress impacts the immune system and its ability to function properly, as well as causing changes in mental processes. Cognitive factors such as negative beliefs about self, the world in general, and the future can impact whether or not a person becomes depressed. Finally, behavior such as social withdrawal, inability to cope effectively, and feeling trapped will influence a person's susceptibility to depression.

There are also "relieving factors" that will impact depressive symptoms in the opposite way by lessening the probability that depression will emerge. For example, improving one's social circumstances, receiving good social support, and having the opportunity for a fresh start can all help a vulnerable person to fight depression. Psychological factors such as improved self-esteem, better coping skills, and working through problems are examples of relieving factors that will help someone avoid depression. Finally, biological factors can also be improved and help with the physical side of depression. Taking appropriate medications, sleeping well, receiving enough light (especially for seasonal affective disorder), exercising, and having appropriate and healthy nutrition will help a person avoid or improve a depressive state.

In discussing the different approaches and theories relative to depression, it is important to remember that no two patients are exactly alike—even with the same disorder. We can certainly learn and apply ideas from one patient to another, but each patient is always unique. Models and theories can help guide our thoughts about depression, but using the "cookie-cutter" approach that tries to force a patient into a specific category without appreciating their individuality must be avoided. The same rule applies when considering a treatment approach: the treatment must fit the disorder *and* the individual patient.

3

❖

The Different Types and Manifestations of Depression

INTRODUCTION

Although most people think that they know what "depression" is, the experience of depression is unique for each individual and is complicated by the fact that there are many different types of depression with different causes, courses or patterns, results, and treatments. However, there are some shared characteristics and symptoms such as persistent sadness, anxiety, or an "empty" feeling that are found in most types of depression. Patients also may feel as though there is nothing that they could have done to prevent getting depressed, and they often feel guilty without knowing why, and may feel at a loss for not having been able to prevent the depression.

A prominent symptom of depression is "anhedonia," which means the absence of pleasure in doing things that had previously been enjoyable. A loss of interest in hobbies or recreational activities can be a result of feeling so fatigued and "empty" that affected individuals can't muster the energy to do much of anything. Even things like recreation, social activities, and sex are not experienced as pleasurable. This is often very frustrating to those who are trying to motivate and be supportive of a depressed person; efforts along these lines will not only probably fail but the depressed person will most likely resent those who try to force them to become active.

In addition to being physically fatigued, the depressed person frequently complains of feeling mentally slowed down as well. Difficulty in concentrating, remembering, making decisions, and even thinking are quite common. This type of cognitive inefficiency is sometimes described by depressed people as "losing their mind," and feeling like they will never be "normal" again. This is perhaps one of the most frightening aspects about depression—a fear that it will never go away.

Invariably people with depression report sleep problems in a variety of different forms. The most typical type of insomnia is when a person takes a long time to fall asleep or awakens frequently during the night having never achieved a consistently restful sleep. Some depressed persons find they awaken earlier than usual (by several hours) and cannot get back to sleep. Others experience "hypersomnia" where they sleep longer than needed. Sometimes even 10–12 hours or more of sleep will result in awakening and still feeling exhausted. Too much or too little sleep can cause a depressed person to still feel tired and to have no energy or motivation to do much but stay in bed.

Different forms of food and weight problems are also typically found in those who are depressed. Patients report having no appetite, no desire to eat and thus losing weight, or eating compulsively or binging and gaining weight. Overeating does not usually include wisely chosen or nutritious food items; overconsuming simple carbohydrates and sugars as well as high fat foods usually results in weight gain.

Depressed people, particularly men, are more likely to drink alcohol abusively; this is called "self-medicating." This type of situation can be referred to as a "chicken or the egg" problem, because while depression might lead to alcohol or drug abuse, alcohol and drug abuse might lead to depression. Professional providers must obtain a clear clinical history and a good time line as to when the patient's problems or symptoms first began to emerge in order to understand an individual's situation.

Additional symptoms common to depression are morbid and persistent (sometimes obsessive) thoughts of death, dying, and/or suicide. A depressed person is higher risk for suicide, and the level of risk must be assessed during the evaluation and at subsequent appointments. Behaviorally, depressed people will sometimes withdraw and become socially isolated, reducing their activity level and their social involvement. They are often restless and irritable, and are rarely pleasant to be around. Initially, friends/family may try to help someone who appears to be hurting, but when nothing seems to work, others begin to avoid them, leading to feelings of worthlessness and the sense that no one really cares about them.

Perhaps the symptoms of depression that will most likely lead a person to seek help are persistent and often vague physical complaints that have not responded to conventional medical treatment. It is not usually depression that brings the person in for an appointment with their physician but rather one or more of an extensive list of persistent physical symptoms such as headaches, digestive disorders, chronic pain, sexual dysfunction, muscular-skeletal problems, sleep problems, and many other physical complaints. It can mean that these symptoms surfaced due to depression, although it is often the physical symptoms that are first noticed by a health professional.

DIFFERENT TYPES OF DEPRESSION

Unipolar Depression

Unipolar depression refers to depression that is only manifest in one direction—negative mood states; bipolar disorder is discussed later in this chapter. Unipolar depression means that the depression is the primary type of symptom pattern.

Major Depressive Disorder (MDD)

In order to be diagnosed with any type of depression, the person must experience at least five of the following symptoms, and they *must* have either depressed mood or loss of interest/pleasure or both; in addition, the symptoms must not be due to a medical condition. For the diagnosis of MDD these symptoms must be present during the same two-week period and be a change from the way the person was functioning prior to the onset of symptoms. Symptoms of major depressive disorder (most of the day, and on most days) include:

1. Depressed mood (in children or teens, this could be an irritable mood)
2. Diminished pleasure or interest (anhedonia)
3. Significant weight loss when not dieting or weight gain; or a decrease in appetite
4. Insomnia or hypersomnia
5. Psychomotor retardation or agitation
6. Fatigue or decreased energy
7. Feelings of worthlessness or excessive guilt
8. Decreased ability to think, concentrate, and make decisions
9. Recurrent ideas about death and suicide

Dysthymic Disorder (DD)

MDD has symptoms that interfere with the ability to work, study, sleep, eat, and enjoy previously pleasurable activities. It may occur only once, or it can occur numerous times throughout a person's lifetime. Dysthymic disorder is typically a long-term, chronic disorder in which the symptoms do not disable but do keep one from functioning optimally or feeling good. Some people who have DD can experience episodes of MDD, and when they occur together this is referred to as "double depression," which is not an "official" diagnosis but is commonly used to describe the co-existence of MDD and DD.

In order to be diagnosed with DD, a person must feel depressed most of the day, and on most days, and must have continued for at least two years. Interestingly, people with DD frequently do not realize they are depressed because they have felt like this for so long that it feels "normal to them." Frequently, when they receive treatment and start to improve they realize that it has been a long time since they have truly felt normal—that is to say, appropriately happy or sad depending on the circumstances.

In addition to the symptom of feeling depressed most of the time, a diagnosis of DD requires that the person must exhibit at least two of the following symptoms for at least two years (one year for children) and not be symptom free for longer than two months:

1. Poor appetite or overeating
2. Hypersomnia or insomnia
3. Decreased energy or fatigue
4. Diminished self-esteem
5. Poor concentration and difficulty in decision-making
6. Feelings of hopelessness

Atypical Depression (AD)

Atypical depression is found in about 30–40 percent of depressed patients, sharing many of the usual symptoms of depression and with a few differences. For example, they may have pleasurable experiences in certain specific and key areas of their life. Also, they usually don't have sleep problems or loss of appetite. In fact, some patients tend to overeat and oversleep. Some of the common symptoms of AD are

- General sadness that can be broken with pleasurable activities

- Feelings of rejection—usually very strong
- A sensation of heaviness; especially in the arms
- Strong preference for carbohydrates and possible overeating on "junk food"

The symptoms of AD are debilitating, although they may not seem as severe as those in MDD. Episodes of AD are usually shorter but more frequent than those of MDD.

Adjustment Disorder with Depressed Mood (ADDM)

This disorder is not actually grouped with the mood disorders but is in a different category—the adjustment disorders. An adjustment disorder includes emotional or behavioral symptoms that emerge as a response to an identifiable stressor that has occurred within three months prior to the onset of the symptoms. These symptoms are clinically significant insofar as they produce marked distress and are in excess of what might be expected as a normal response to the stressors in question. There also needs to be significant impairment in normal social and/or occupational (academic) functioning. In the case of adjustment disorder with depressed mood, the significant symptoms are the same as we would see in other depressive disorders. However, in this case the symptoms are clearly in response to a specific stressor, and the depressive symptoms are not due to another depressive disorder. Adjustment disorders can be acute or chronic as well. A chronic adjustment disorder is a situation when the stressor does not disappear and the person continues to be exposed to it and continues to react to it with depression.

Depressive Personality Disorder (DPD)

This disorder shows a pervasive pattern of depressive cognitions that begin at least by early adulthood and usually well before that. The person will present at least five of the following symptoms:

1. The typical mood is dominated by feelings of dejection, gloominess, cheerlessness, joylessness, and unhappiness.
2. Their self-concept centers on beliefs of inadequacy, worthlessness, and low self-esteem.
3. They are critical, blaming, and derogatory toward themselves.
4. They are brooding and tend to worry.
5. They are negativistic, critical, and judgmental toward others.

6. They are pessimistic.
7. They are prone to feeling guilty or remorseful.

This diagnostic category can be confusing since it may appear similar to early-onset dysthymic disorder. In fact some professionals say that there is no meaningful distinction between the two disorders. However, others feel that the chronic attitudes of pessimism, negativism, hopelessness, and dejection that are found consistently over time in persons with depressive personality disorder cannot be adequately explained by the dysregulation of mood as would be the case in dysthymic disorder.

Other Forms of Depressive Disorders

Seasonal Affective Disorder (SAD)

People who suffer from SAD begin to experience mood difficulties when the days become shorter with less light, and they tend to show improvement in spring when days are brighter and longer. Although many people experience an increase of emotional problems in winter when days are short and gray, people with SAD have clear symptoms of depression and it should not be ignored. A number of effective treatments for SAD include psychotherapy, medication, and increased real or artificial sunlight. With appropriate treatment or efforts at prevention, people with SAD can function normally and get through the winter without undue complications.

Premenstrual Dysphoric Disorder (PMDD)

Premenstrual syndrome (PMS) has been discussed for decades in the professional literature and even longer among women. People joke about it, dismiss it as nonsense, or simply ignore it, but 80 percent of women report at least mild premenstrual symptoms and 20–50 percent report moderate to severe symptoms. The symptoms can include dysphoric (depressed) mood, irritability, sleep disturbances, labile (changeable) mood, and others. PMS symptoms usually appear a week or so before the woman's period and usually subside about a week later. In most women PMS is more of an annoyance than a problem, but for some it can be very severe.

About 5 percent of women have premenstrual symptoms so severe that for at least several days during each cycle they will experience significant difficulty with daily and social functioning. If this condition improves as menstruation commences and ends, and there is no other diagnosis that more appropriately fits the symptom patterns, then we refer to this more severe type as premenstrual dysphoric disorder. To qualify for this diagnosis a woman must experience the symptoms for most of her periods over the past year and must have at least five of the more serious symptoms of depression. PMDD is highly treatable, but women often do not seek treatment because PMDD symptoms disappear monthly on their own (although typically return), it may be embarrassing to discuss, or they are not aware that treatment is available.

Postpartum Depression (PPD)

Some women experience severe mood changes following the birth of a child. It is estimated that at least 40 percent of live births in this country are complicated by postpartum mood disorders (*postpartum* means after the birth of a child). These mood changes can be very mild and pass in a few hours or days and are referred to as the "baby blues." While this is not an official diagnosis, most mothers and physicians are familiar with the term and its meaning. A small percentage of women experience a severe condition known as postpartum psychosis that may require hospitalization. A slightly larger group (about 10–15 percent of women) experience postpartum depression. This is a debilitating condition that affects not only the mother but others in the family including the new baby. PPD is a highly treatable condition that responds well to appropriate care such as medication and/or psychotherapy.

Depressive Disorders Accompanying Other Conditions

As mentioned earlier, *comorbidity* refers to a condition when a person suffers from more than one disorder at the same time. This can be either psychological or medical conditions or both and can complicate diagnosis and treatment. There are several medical and psychological problems that put a person at higher risk for depression, as well as situations where depression can result from medical conditions or from medications.

Psychological Comorbid Conditions

Depression can and often does accompany a number of different "mental" disorders. For example, depression is common in alcohol and substance abuse disorders and in many anxiety disorders including panic disorder, phobias, general anxiety disorder, posttraumatic stress disorder, and obsessive-compulsive disorder. It is also common in somatic symptom disorder, eating disorders, personality disorders, and grief/bereavement.

One of the most common and serious comorbid conditions for depression is anxiety. It is estimated that one-half of people with MDD also suffer from an anxiety disorder.

Why are anxiety and depression so similar? Although there is considerable speculation, there is no agreed-upon conclusion except for the following statements:

- Depression and anxiety seem to co-exist in many people.
- The co-occurrence of these two conditions complicates diagnosis and treatment of both.
- Appropriate treatments seem to improve both conditions.

Another disorder that is comorbid with depression is attention deficit/hyperactivity disorder (ADHD) and attention deficit disorder (ADD); this is true for children, adolescents, and adults. Typically, it is thought that the frustrations, continuing failures, and stigma of ADD and ADHD can lead people to become depressed. However, it has also been demonstrated that people with ADD and ADHD can suffer from depression for reasons other than feeling discouraged about having the ADD or ADHD.

MEDICAL FACTORS IN DEPRESSION

Medical Conditions and Depression

Some medical conditions are frequently comorbid with depression, and their treatment depends in part on the treatment of the depression. Some of the medical conditions that frequently involve depression are stroke, Alzheimer's disease, Parkinson's disease, diabetes, coronary artery disease, cancer, fibromyalgia, chronic fatigue syndrome, and asthma. The following reasons indicate why depression emerges following the diagnosis of a medical disease:

- Psychological reactions to the diagnosis
- Chronic pain and/or impairment
- Direct or indirect effects of their illness on the brain
- Triggered by certain medications used to treat the illness

Other conditions that frequently lead to depression are Huntington's disease and hormonal disorders like hypothyroidism, which manifests symptoms similar to depression. Cushing's disease may cause depression because it affects the adrenal glands, which leads to symptoms like depression. Any person who has one of these conditions is higher risk for depression than someone in the general population. In fact, depression is found at higher rates in people with any serious illness.

Two conditions that are frequently linked to depression are cancer and cardiovascular disease. As far back as the 1950s patients with a rapidly progressing cancer experienced more depression and anxiety, and especially among those with the most severe illnesses and the shortest life expectancy. It has also been found that cancer patients who just "give up" have a worse prognosis than those who keep fighting. Research has demonstrated clear relationships between how people respond to cancer and cancer treatment and their emotional state, although this is very complex and not well understood. Others have concluded that there is no obvious connection between emotional health and cancer, while others believe that cancer patients whose emotional and psychological needs are managed effectively are most likely to be receptive to support and activities in their environments. Most would agree that providing more and better services to cancer patients is beneficial in all cases.

In terms of coronary heart disease, numerous studies demonstrate that depression negatively affects patients following a heart attack. Some have reported that heart patients who are depressed are more likely to experience more complications, to develop more serious cardiac disease, or to die sooner. Although this sounds ominous, becoming depressed following a major reversal in one's health status is quite normal. The key is that, when a patient with a serious disease like cancer or cardiovascular illness becomes depressed, the depression as well as the primary illness must be treated. In fact, it is assumed that if the depressive condition is being treated, the increased risks are neutralized.

Medications and Depression

Some medications can cause the development or worsening of depressive symptoms, and it is important to be aware of mood changes that occur while taking these medications in order to determine if the changes may be due to the drugs. Many medications that are used to treat cardiovascular conditions can cause depressive-like symptoms. For example, a very common side effect of these types of medications that is similar to depression is lethargy, but people may also notice mood changes. Hormonal agents, including birth control pills and steroids, as well as some anti-inflammatory drugs and anti-infective agents can lead to depressive symptoms.

Some psychiatric medications like tranquilizers and antipsychotic drugs and medications used to treat Parkinson's disease can also lead to depressive symptoms. Energizing drugs like cocaine and methamphetamine can often cause depression when a person is withdrawing from a drug or when the drug begins to wear off. Some stimulant drugs like Ritalin are often used to treat conditions like ADD and ADHD and have similar risks for depression.

For the majority of patients, any of the above-mentioned legal drugs can be used safely and effectively under the supervision of a physician. Mood or behavior changes that appear after taking a new medication must be reported to the physician immediately. The doctor can then make adjustments or change to another drug that might not have the same side effects.

BIPOLAR DISORDER

Bipolar disorder (BPD) has been recognized for a very long time as a serious mental disturbance. It used to be referred to as "manic-depressive disease," and many people still use that label. Although most professionals consider it a type of mood disorder, some consider it a type of serious mental illness similar to schizophrenia, although that is not the prevailing opinion.

The onset of BPD usually occurs earlier in life than depression, even during childhood, although it can occasionally emerge later in adulthood with women tending to have later onset than men. BPD is a recurrent condition, and about two-thirds of people with BPD who recover from an acute episode will experience additional episodes of depression, mania, or both. The average number of episodes in a patient's life is four, although this can vary considerably from patient to patient. Unlike unipolar depression, BPD affects men and women equally, although men tend to show more mania and women more depression. BPD involves mood extremes, depression and mania, and these represent dramatic changes from the person's normal mood state. *Mania* refers to extremes in behavior that are completely different from depression. A person who is experiencing mania is very active—sometimes almost frantic, does not sleep much, has racing and seemingly unconnected thoughts, is impulsive and shows poor judgment, and displays disturbed speech and behavior. A milder form of mania called "hypomania" is not as extreme and disorganized as mania. The two main types of BPD are bipolar disorder I, which involves episodes of major depression and mania, and bipolar II disorder, which includes typically milder forms of depression and hypomania.

In order to be diagnosed with BPD the patient must demonstrate both depressive and manic (or hypomanic) symptoms. If only depression is present it is not considered BPD but rather a form of unipolar depression; it is rare that a person presents only manic symptoms. As with depression, BPD can be comorbid with other disorders. One disturbing but important fact is that 50 percent of people with BPD have a co-occurring substance abuse disorder.

The manic episode is an important diagnostic feature of BPD and involves a period of abnormally and persistently elevated moods. The person in a manic state usually has episodes of extremely restless energy and cannot relax. They often experience dramatic mood swings that cause issues at home and at work or in other settings. Although it is not likely that anyone would present with all of the following symptoms, some that are seen in mania include

- Feelings of grandiosity or inflated self-esteem
- Diminished need for sleep
- Increased talkativeness
- Racing thoughts
- Easily distracted
- Increased productivity at work or school
- Increased involvement in high-risk activities
- Often use bad judgment

Some additional symptoms are

- Abnormal or excessive elation
- Unusual irritability
- Increased sex drive
- Increased energy
- Inappropriate social behavior

We often think of mania or hypomania as being excited or ecstatic— almost joyous. However, some people with this disorder will exhibit irritability and anger rather than euphoria or excitement. While true mania is often quite dramatic and even bizarre, hypomania is sometimes not as easy to recognize. The following are the most common manifestations of hypomania:

- Less sleep
- More energy and strength

- More self-confidence
- Increased activity levels, including work
- Enjoying work more than usual
- More socially active
- Spending too much money
- Make more plans and have many new ideas
- Less shy and inhibited
- More talkative than usual
- Increased sex drive
- Increased consumption of coffee, cigarettes, and alcohol
- Overly optimistic
- Increased laughing
- Thinking fast/sudden ideas

While the patient may not experience all of these symptoms, it is important to realize that the symptoms they present are a change from their normal functioning.

Bipolar disorder is a mood disorder that represents significant and problematic departures from normal mood states. It involves depression but not unipolar depression and can create a significant disease burden on patients, families, employers, and society. However, bipolar disorder is usually a highly treatable condition with appropriate medications and psychotherapy.

When previously discussing MDD, I also mentioned a related condition called dysthymic disorder (DD). The symptoms of DD are less acute or severe than in MDD but have a long and continuous history that typically goes back many years. In BPD a similar condition with a long and consistent history is called cyclothymic disorder (CTD). According to the *Diagnostic and Statistical Manual* the following are the diagnostic criteria for CTD:

A. For at least two years (one year in children and adolescents) the patient displays episodes of hypomanic symptoms as well as depressive symptoms, and the depression does not meet the criteria for a major depressive episode.
B. During the above two-year period (one year in children or adolescents) the patient has not experienced an absence of symptoms in criterion A for more than two months at a time.
C. During the two-year period of the disturbance there has not been a major depressive episode, a manic episode, or a mixed episode.

D. The symptoms of criterion A are not better accounted for by schizoaffective disorder, schizophrenia, schizophreniform disorder, delusional disorder, or psychotic disorder not otherwise specified.
E. The symptoms are not due to the direct physiological effects of substances (drug abuse or medications) or another medical condition.
F. The symptoms cause clinically significant distress or impairment in social, occupational, academic, or other important areas of functioning.

SUMMARY

Depression is manifested in many forms and can be caused by different factors. It can accompany other psychological or medical conditions and can make these comorbid conditions more difficult to manage and to treat. There is no reason for a person with any type of depression or mood disorder to suffer in silence—there are many avenues for help and treatment. Too often people with serious medical conditions view their depressive symptoms as an annoying, unavoidable byproduct of being ill, but these symptoms and mood disorders in general should be treated—this will also help the person deal with their comorbid illnesses and will make treatment for each condition more effective.

4

❖

Gender and Depression

INTRODUCTION

Historically women were expected to experience more emotional problems and men to have more behavioral, substance-related, and legal difficulties. To evaluate the validity of these beliefs we will examine the research literature and discuss the differences between the sexes with respect to depression.

One in every four to five women develops depression at some time during their lives and most will experience recurrent episodes. Depression affects a woman's ability to fulfill normal daily responsibilities including family and work, and research demonstrates that the young children of depressed mothers have impaired cognitive and emotional development. However, appropriate treatment can help mothers and their children with difficulties that are the result of the mother's depression.

Most research demonstrates that about twice as many women as men are affected by depressive conditions each year in the United States and in most other developed countries. In developing countries there has not been much research done on mental health issues as yet, and some of the few studies that have been done have not shown much difference between men and women with respect to the frequency of depression. Since research, treatment, and the availability of services are often minimal in less-developed countries, it is difficult to determine the significance of these early findings. However, in most developed countries (with few exceptions) this two-to-one ratio (women to men) is quite consistent for all types of depression. The World Health Organization (WHO) reports that mental illness disability falls most heavily upon those, predominantly women, who have three or more medical and/or psychological conditions. The risk factors that disproportionately affect women include gender-based violence, socioeconomic disadvantage, low income or income inequality, low or subordinate social status, and responsibility for the care of others.

The gender difference in depression only occurs in the years between puberty and menopause; before and after this part of life there appears to be no difference in the rates of depression between men and women. This, understandably, has led many to assume that gender-based depression rates are hormonally linked, and we will discuss this later in this chapter. Patient gender significantly modifies the clinical features of depression, and men and women tend to report different types of symptoms. It is clear that gender impacts depression but also that depression affects men and women differently. The reasons are not yet clear, but over the past couple of decades new theories and studies have improved our understanding of how and why men and women are affected differently by depressive disorders.

THEORIES REGARDING GENDER DIFFERENCES IN DEPRESSION

Artifact Theory

Some professionals believe that the difference in the rates of depression for men and women is just an artifact; there is no real reason medically or psychologically why more women than men report depression. This suggests, therefore, that clinicians often fail to detect depression in men because they tend to hide their feelings from doctors/providers. Although women may be reluctant to discuss depression with their providers, the research does suggest that men are probably more frequently "underdetected" when it comes to depression.

Hormone Theory

Many speculate that hormones may be responsible for the differential rates of depression for men and women; this would indicate that hormonal changes can trigger depression in many women. This theory is particularly compelling when it is noted that the gender difference for depression only holds between puberty and menopause, as noted above. It also could explain why women are prone to other types of depression such as post-partum depression, premenstrual dysphoric disorder, and PMS. Yet, many feel that this explanation is too simplistic, and many researchers say it is unlikely that hormone changes alone are responsible for the higher rates of depression in women. For example, many important and stress-filled events that women experience occur at and during puberty, pregnancy, and menopause. It is also true that hormone levels alone are not very good predictors of depression.

Rumination Theory

Susan Nolen-Hoeksema, who has studied gender differences in depression for many years, has contributed compelling ideas about gender and depression. She finds that some depressed people tend to repeatedly think about and dwell on their feelings and to continually consider the causes and consequences of their depression; she calls this "rumination." She reports that people who ruminate when they are sad are more likely to become depressed and are more likely to remain depressed longer. She also finds that women are more likely than men to be ruminators and are therefore more likely to become depressed.

Societal Pressure Theory

Almost from birth women in Western cultures are taught to seek an unrealistically low body weight and slender body shape within a society where cultural standards for men's appearance are more lenient. As girls enter adolescence increased pressure to look a particular way can lead to girls and young women showing more dissatisfaction with their own bodies. This, too, is the period of time when gender differences in depression begin to emerge and when young women will most likely develop eating disorders as well as depression. The point of this theory is that society places different levels of stress on women regarding their appearance and behavior, beginning most significantly at puberty and continuing through adulthood. Perhaps it is not hormones but rather cultural pressure that can lead women to depression more often than men.

Lack of Control Theory

Women are thought to be more prone to depression because many women feel that they have little control over their lives. Research finds that women are also more likely to develop learned helplessness and feel victimized, both of which often lead to feelings of helplessness and/or depression. Women are more often the victims of sexual assault, rape, domestic violence, and child sexual abuse; these forms of abuse and violence can lead to feelings of a lack of control and helplessness that can also lead to depression. Other cultural patterns can lead to feelings of limited or no control over a woman's own life, including such things as educational or occupational discrimination, caretaker responsibilities, etc.

Self-Blame Theory

Women are more likely to blame their failures on their own lack of ability and attribute their successes just to luck, which is a style of thinking that is linked to depression. These differences are noted in the early teens when the different rates of depression between boys and girls begin to emerge. Clearly, if a person attributes their success to factors other than their own skill and ability, and their failure primarily to their own shortcomings, they will draw little pleasure from success and will blame themselves for failure. While this pattern may lead to depression, it is not likely that this is the only factor that differentiates men from women with respect to depression.

Quality of Life and Cultural Theory

In general, more women around the world live in poverty, perform more menial jobs, have less than adequate housing, and experience more discrimination than men, and these are all factors that are related to higher rates of depression. In addition, most cultures and subcultures place the majority of housework and child care responsibilities on women, an obvious source of stress. Women tend to be the primary caregivers in a family, including caring for the acute and chronically ill family members as well as the elderly, which is, of course, yet another source of stress in their lives.

As more women with family care responsibilities enter the work force, they often experience a decrease in the quality and quantity of leisure time. Young married women caring for small children are especially at risk for depression, as are women who are more often rejected for developing mental illness. In many cultures women are often expected to care for a mentally ill husband; however, if the wife becomes mentally ill she is often returned to her family, deserted, or divorced. Some cultures require arranged marriages, forced abortions, and genital mutilation of women, all of which place women at more risk for depression.

SEXUAL VIOLENCE, REPRODUCTIVE HEALTH, AND DEPRESSION

Sexual Violence and Depression

We know that the harmful impact of sexual violence and abuse in childhood leads to mental health problems in adulthood, and depression is one of the most common reactions. The WHO reports that the lifetime prevalence rate for violence against women ranges from 16 to 50 percent, depending upon the study and its locale, and that about 20 percent of all women suffer rape or attempted rape at some time during their life. Since women are more likely to be victims of sexual violence, they also experience more depression as a result of the trauma of sexual victimization. Although women are most frequently the victims of sexual violence and the resultant mental health problems, some studies found that male survivors of sexual abuse suffered very severe psychological consequences and also suffered more complex problems later in their lives. Although sexual abuse and violence primarily affect women, men are certainly not immune to the difficulties that result from this problem.

Reproductive Health Issues and Depression

Women are twice as likely to experience depression and other emotional problems during their reproductive years (typically 25–45), and there is a high frequency of depression during premenstrual, perimenopausal, and immediately postpartum periods.

Premenstrual Syndrome (PMS) refers to physical and emotional symptoms that a woman experiences usually during the week prior to the onset of menstruation. It is estimated that 3–4 percent of women suffer PMS severe enough to interfere with work and social functioning. A related condition that is even more problematic is premenstrual dysphoric disorder (PMDD), which is a diagnostic category characterized by depressed mood, marked anxiety, mood swings, and decreased interest in normal activities. These severe symptoms are similar to major depressive disorder, but the condition is much briefer since it tends to improve following the cessation of the woman's menstrual flow.

Another issue relative to a woman's emotional well-being and her susceptibility to depression is reproductive tract surgery. This type of surgery may impact a woman's mental health due to the identification of the reproductive organs with her sexuality and feminine identity. Inadequate professional concerns about the psychological impact on women who have had reproductive tract surgeries such as hysterectomies and tubal ligations may lead to adverse mental health consequences, depression being the most common. Bladder control problems, which are more common in women, are apt to lead to emotional disturbances and depression as well.

Postpartum Depression

Women all over the world suffer from postpartum depression (PPD) and their symptoms are frequently ignored and untreated. Some research demonstrates that between 10–28 percent of mothers experience a major depressive episode during the postpartum period, although larger studies tend to find rates closer to 10 percent. Most of the research on PPD is done in industrialized countries, but we do know that PPD has been detected in developing countries at a higher rate than expected and has a severe impact on a mother's health and that of her baby; very frequently PPD sufferers are not provided with appropriate treatment.

Although professionals focus more attention on PPD today than in the past, it is still frequently overlooked. PPD is often missed at the primary care level because providers are typically more concerned with the infant's health, and problems may go unnoticed in the mother. It might also be that the mother may be too embarrassed or unaware to raise the issue of depression since she is expected to feel happy rather than sad during this wonderful time. However, PPD is a serious condition for both the mother and the baby, and it should not be ignored. Maternal PPD may affect mother-baby bonding and could possibly affect the child's later development. Substantial research has found that children of mothers who had PPD are at a higher risk for psychological problems later in life.

Some studies find that not only can PPD affect mother-infant interactions but also that a mother with PPD is more likely to develop negative attitudes toward the infant and to report that the infant is more difficult and demanding than do mothers who have not suffered from PPD. Children of mothers with PPD are more likely to have behavioral problems such as difficulties sleeping and eating, tantrums, hyperactivity, delays in mental development, emotional and social difficulties, and early onset of depression themselves.

There are a number of factors that will cause a mother to develop PPD, but women of all ages, socioeconomic classes, and races or ethnic backgrounds can be affected by PPD. Any woman who was pregnant, delivered a baby in the past few months, miscarried, or weaned a child from breast feeding can develop PPD. The best single predictor of PPD is a prior history of depression. Another significant risk factor is a family history of depression and/or PPD.

Things that also contribute to the risk for PPD, even if the mother does not have a prior history of depression, include anxiety disorders prior to pregnancy and other problems like a history of substance abuse prior to pregnancy. Some additional factors that increase risk for PPD include

- Poor social support
- Adverse events during the postpartum period
- Marital instability
- Young maternal age
- Infants with health problems or perceived "difficult" temperaments

MEN AND DEPRESSION

Since depression impacts men less often than women it is not surprising that most of the research focuses on women. During the 19th century, when "being a danger to society" was the main criterion for someone being confined to a mental hospital, men were more often committed to asylums than women. In the past century there has been a change from "violence" to an emphasis on "illness" as the basis for identifying a mental condition, and now women are more frequently the focus of mental health treatment and hospitalization.

Today the more dangerous and violent mentally ill patients are typically placed in jails or prisons rather than hospitals and, unfortunately, men may be even less likely to be identified as needing mental health treatment than they were in the past. One noticeable trend in developed countries is that low income women often develop depression, but the men are more likely to turn to alcohol, drugs, and violence.

Often men will not, or perhaps cannot, identify their feelings with any certainty or assurance. They may describe symptoms of depression without realizing they are depressed. Men are more reluctant to seek help for many reasons, including the fear that colleagues and superiors at work might discover their "weakness," possibly leading to negative repercussions. Men tend to hide their emotions and suppress or resist showing affection—especially to other men. Occasionally, men refuse to use their health insurance to pay for mental health treatment, preferring to pay out of pocket rather than taking the chance that someone may discover they are seeking treatment.

The reluctance of men to admit needing or seeking help for mental health problems is unfortunately found for medical problems as well. At every age men experience poorer health and have a higher death rate than women. When men are experiencing emotional problems they tend to keep it to themselves, but the gender difference in seeking help cannot be the only factor involved in the gender difference in depression. Regardless of the reasons why depression is not detected as frequently in men as in women, this can create a dangerous situation as we know that men have a higher rate of committing suicide and a higher rate of cardiovascular disease than women, and depression leads to a higher risk for both. While depression increases the risk for coronary heart disease in both men and women, it is men who suffer a higher death rate from this condition. Some studies demonstrate that men who report clinical depression are more prone to coronary heart disease and myocardial infarction (heart attack) even a decade later. A tentative explanation for this increased mortality in men includes findings that men are less equipped to deal with feelings of hopelessness and depression than women, and women are more likely to admit their feelings to others including to health care providers. Women are also more likely to accept help and support from others when feeling depressed.

While we know that women in childbearing years have a depression rate twice that of men, there are still at least six million men who suffer from depression in the United States today. Men do not readily admit to being depressed or ask for help, and doctors are less likely to suspect depression in a male when seeing them for a different medical condition. Also, depression in men is often masked by drugs, alcohol, or overworking, and it is often disguised as irritability, anger, or discouragement. Although some men believe that they don't go to as many doctor appointments as women because they are healthier, this is not true. In fact, the real reason has more to do with a discrepancy between a need for care and help-seeking behavior in men; both poor and rich men are less likely than women to report a recent contact with a health care provider. When female college students are depressed they tend to reach out to roommates and friends, and tend to seek nurturing relationships. When male students are depressed they tend to isolate socially and occasionally become outright hostile. Men more often resort to self-medication with drugs and/or alcohol.

A phenomenon called "gender-role conflict" may be part of the reason why men are so reluctant to seek help. Gender role conflict means that men are socialized to be strong, self-reliant, etc., but in reality they have fears, vulnerabilities, and other problems as well. The conflict emerges when men feel they cannot seek help or support when they need it because it would not be considered "masculine behavior." Traditional male roles are often considered oppressive to women, but some argue very con-vincingly that the male role is oppressive to men too.

Work stress and work uncertainty are major sources of stress for many men; not knowing what the future holds, not knowing where you or the organization are going, and not having future career development plans are often serious issues. Other concerns such as not knowing what may be expected of you in the future, not knowing what your boss/colleagues think about your ability, and receiving vague and unclear instructions can create stress as well. Both men and women report that conflicts between family and job responsibilities produce stress, but it seems that men are more negatively affected by this than are women—except for single moth-ers who often experience significant problems with work/family conflict.

The main problem for depressed males is having someone recognize their condition and then receiving appropriate treatment, a much more complicated process than it appears. This suggests that screening for de-pression may be more important for men than for women since women are more likely to self-refer and to be more aware of their emotions. Although antidepressant medications are equally effective for men and women, the sexual side effects that some men experience, like erectile dysfunction (ED), decreased libido (sex drive), or delayed or absent orgasm lead men to stop taking the medications too soon. Since 40–60 percent of men in the 40–60 age range experience ED, and one of the common causes of ED is depression, avoiding antidepressant medications is not the correct choice. However, if the medication used to treat depression causes ED or other side effects, then treatment compliance can become a serious issue. Rather than discontinuing the medication on his own, the patient needs to discuss the side effects with his physician, who can change dosages, prescribe a different medication, or add a medication to help ED. It is important that men understand that when treatment produces some un-welcome side effects, like ED, it does not mean treatment should be stopped, but rather that treatment may need to be modified.

GENDER AND SUICIDE

With respect to gender issues and suicide, there are some differences that bear examination, but, as we know, depression is a significant risk factor for both men and women with women reporting attempted suicides 2–3 times more often than men. In fact self-inflicted injury, including suicide, ranks ninth out of the 10 leading causes of disease burden for females age five and older worldwide. However, men are four times more likely to die by suicide than women. The WHO finds that, with the exception of China and parts of India, men commit suicide more often than women, and the world rate is 3.5:1. However, it is also reported from other international studies that women attempt suicide more frequently than do men.

Some believe that women are more likely to attempt suicide as a "cry for help" or as an attention-seeking device, while men attempt suicide with the intent of killing themselves. Although this may occasionally be true, it is unlikely that this simple explanation can account for patterns found throughout so many different cultures. Failed suicide attempts by males are probably not reported as often as those by females because men are less likely to reach out to friends, family, or professionals when they need help, and this is also a pattern commonly found in many cultures.

Regardless of whether a person is really trying to kill him- or herself or is seeking attention, a suicide attempt should never be ignored. Most people who attempt suicide probably do not want to die—they just want to escape the pain they are living with. They need someone to help them generate options that offer some hope of relief. Friends and family can assist with support and direction, but this serious and potentially tragic situation needs to be handled by trained and experienced professionals.

SUMMARY

Women are twice as likely as men to develop depression for a variety of reasons. While gender differences as well as hormones do factor into the equation, it is most often a woman experiencing "role overload" that places them in the position where more is expected of them than they can realistically fulfill. For example, work/home conflicts, caregiver burden, single parenting obligations, etc. can create a burden of stress that increases a woman's susceptibility to depression. Social and cultural factors, unequal power and status, and sexual and physical abuse can affect the situation as well. In addition, women tend to ruminate over their difficulties more than men, which also affects their vulnerability for depression.

Those who suffer with different physical and behavioral/emotional disorders are more susceptible to certain disorders like depression. Research demonstrates that boys and girls (or men and women) have the same risk factors for depression but that girls experience more of them during childhood, which makes them more vulnerable in adolescence. Although there are many differences between men and women relative to depression, there are similarities as well. Both become depressed for the same types of reasons and also improve for the same kinds of reasons. However, women are exposed to more risk factors, which results in women developing depression twice as often as men. Looking at cognitive or thinking patterns, women are more likely to hold negative perceptions and thoughts prior to the onset of depression and experience more negative events during the previous year than men.

Another reason for gender differences in the rates of depression is the gender bias in the treatment of mental disorders. The WHO reports that doctors are more likely to diagnose women with depression even when they score the same on tests or present with identical symptoms as men. They also found that, while women have higher levels of distress and are more likely to be diagnosed with emotional problems than men who report the same symptoms, once men discuss their problem with a professional they receive treatment just as often. Clearly, the difference is partly due to the tendency of men not to see or to admit to problems as readily as women.

Articles in women's magazines as well as the health section of the daily paper demonstrate a shift toward the "medicalization" of deviation from women's traditional roles. Meanwhile, a male's depressive illness is increasingly described in terms of problems with work, aggression, or athletics. Women and their problems are more often described from a traditional female role perspective and, thus, are attributed to the difficulties of being a wife or mother; men are seen as getting depressed because they are not performing on the job or on the athletic field. Another result of the "medicalization" of women's depression is treating her condition with medication rather than dealing with the social conditions that are contributing to the problem. This trend does not help restore women to health but rather perpetuates the situations that cause the problem even if there is temporary symptom relief.

There appears to be a gender bias in the diagnosis of mental health problems in general; historically, women who display deviant behavior are labeled "mad" while men displaying deviant behavior are "bad." Today, a normal, healthy adult is usually judged by male norms, which can lead to some interesting complications. A woman who either conforms too closely or rejects the female norms is judged as psychiatrically "ill." As far back as 1961, psychiatrist Thomas Szasz pointed out that the overuse of medical diagnoses and treatments for "problems in living" tended to cloud the frequent issues related to unhappy living conditions, and by "medicalizing" these problems it is very easy to ignore the real problems that cause the disorder in question.

Recognizing that these problems exist is a start, but providing the treatment necessary and making it accessible is the answer to the issues. Men and women both suffer from depression, and treating them appropriately is vitally important. Whatever is responsible for the differences between men and women with respect to depression is not as important as making sure that people suffering from depression are recognized and diagnosed, and that proper treatment is provided in a timely fashion.

5

❖❖❖

Life Cycle Issues
and Depression

INTRODUCTION

The more we learn about depression, the more interesting it becomes, and it is hardly surprising to find that age and developmental level are factors that influence depression and its treatment. Depression in children and adolescents doesn't always present itself like it does in adults or the elderly, and while it is true that all age groups can be victimized by depression, how it appears, its course, the treatment, and results can vary among age groups. Most information mentioned in previous chapters relates primarily to the adult experience of depression. This chapter will concentrate on children, adolescents, and the elderly. Professionals tend to neglect and ignore mental health issues in the elderly, and depression is not always recognized or treated in children and adolescents.

DEPRESSION IN CHILDREN AND ADOLESCENTS

Depression in children and adolescents typically looks different from depression in adults. It may be more difficult to detect and may have symptoms such as irritability more often than sadness. Within this age group depression usually accompanies other disorders like anxiety, ADHD, or behavioral problems. In younger age groups the cause of depression is often uncertain but may include factors such as genetics, traumatic childhood events, and current psychosocial difficulties. Understanding the nature and quality of depression in children and adolescents is important to provide appropriate treatment and to be able to help return their lives to "normal." Substantial research suggests that mood disorders often begin early in life and that dealing effectively with depression in its early stages can reduce the seriousness of and treatment for mental health issues later in life. Depression in childhood can sometimes lead to the development of adult depression, or in some cases childhood depression can continue on into adulthood.

In terms of prevalence, approximately 2–6 percent of children suffer from depression, with the proportion of depressed youngsters increasing with age and showing a sharp rise at the onset of puberty. In preadolescents the proportion of boys to girls who are depressed is about equal; although some studies have shown that preadolescent boys are more likely to be depressed than girls. Most professionals, however, agree that after the onset of puberty, depression becomes more common among girls.

In a national survey of 12- to 17-year-olds, 14 percent of adolescents (about 3.5 million youngsters) reported at least one episode of major depression in their lifetime and 9 percent of adolescents (about 2.2 million youngsters) had a major depressive episode in the past year. During the month prior to the onset of a major depressive episode, depressed youngsters were more likely than nondepressed adolescents to use illicit drugs, cigarettes, and alcohol.

One difficulty with detecting depression in youngsters is that it often does not look similar to depression seen in adults and is frequently missed by parents, teachers, and health professionals. In fact, it has been demonstrated that parents report less depressive symptoms in their children than the children report themselves. This is further complicated by the finding that children and teens not only present different symptoms than do adults, but they also present unique symptom patterns from one another. For example, prepubescent children are usually found to have a greater depressive appearance, more somatic (physical) complaints, psychomotor agitation, separation anxiety, phobias, and hallucinations. However, adolescents show greater anhedonia (lack of pleasure), feelings of hopelessness, hypersomnia, weight changes, increased use of alcohol and drugs, and more serious and dangerous suicide attempts.

The World Health Organization reports that throughout the world, girls tend to report more depression, suicidal ideation, and suicidal attempts than boys, although boys will try to express their depression more often through anger and high-risk behaviors and are more likely to commit suicide. Differing symptom patterns in youngsters makes the accurate diagnosis of mood disorders difficult, including those with bipolar disorder, which has been largely neglected in children and adolescents until very recently.

There is evidence that children are experiencing depression more often now than in the past, but it is not easy to determine if we are simply recognizing it more frequently or if more children are developing depression. Children born since World War II have higher rates of depression, become depressed at earlier ages, and are more likely to commit suicide than adolescents and youth of earlier generations. In the past it was thought that children were not cognitively developed enough to become depressed. However, it has been demonstrated that depressed youngsters are more personally upset, do more poorly in school, and are not as popular with other children.

Factors Related to Depression in Children

Children who feel unimportant or unappreciated are more likely to suffer depression. Similarly, depressed adults are more likely to report physical, emotional, and sexual abuse within their family when they were children and teens than nondepressed adults. Other factors that are linked to childhood depression include family conflict, lack of parental support, neglect, and poor parenting skills and practices. Given these findings it is not surprising that children and adolescents who possess a poor self-image are also more prone to depression. Children who are rated by teachers as being hostile toward other kids are more prone to depression, and hostile children who perceive themselves as unpopular are also more likely to be depressed; in fact there is evidence that not being popular often leads to depression in children. Other data reports there is a strong relationship between peer harassment and cognitive vulnerability to depression in children. This is a problem particularly during mid-childhood to adolescence when peers are so important. When youngsters feel like they are not accepted and valued by their peers, they are more likely to feel badly about themselves and are more susceptible to the kinds of thoughts and feelings that can lead to depression. Physical health is also a risk factor, especially among boys. Among all children, however, early illness, injury, and other physical problems are related to depression later in life.

One finding that is encouraging is that neither family social status nor marital status of parents is solely predictive of depression in children as it can be in adult depression. Also, the increased number of single-parent families today is not a predictor of depression by itself. However, some research indicates that children from lower socioeconomic classes become depressed more frequently than youngsters from middle- or upper-class families. This suggests that living at a lower socioeconomic level carries with it the likelihood of being exposed to additional risk factors for depression.

Cognitive variables such as feeling incompetent or incapable, feelings of hopelessness, and erroneous thinking patterns are also related to childhood depression. Youngsters who exhibit behavior problems are anxious and dependent, have school problems (including not progressing normally), use additional school services, and are prone to depression. Insomnia is also a greater risk for depression among young men as they transition to adolescence and adulthood.

Older children and adolescents whose mothers are depressed are 5–6 times more likely to develop depression than their peers. In related studies it is reported that depression in a parent more than doubles the risk for anxiety disorders in children, and this is also true of depression and addictive disorders. More optimistically, the treatment of parental depression can prevent or relieve depression in their children—when the parent(s) improve, so do the children.

Among the more traumatic family circumstances, the loss of a parent, and especially the mother, can lead to later episodes of major depression in children; however, increased family conflict is more commonly related to a higher risk. Generally, the whole family environment is a key factor in the later development of depression for children and adolescents.

One problem that can lead to and/or coexist with depression in children and adolescents is eating disorders, which primarily affect girls and young women. Young women are often exposed to unrealistic examples of what an "attractive" body should look like and can become dissatisfied with their appearance, which can lead to eating disorders and depression.

Depression in children and adolescents seems to be well established as an unfortunate reality of today's mental health climate. Depression in childhood may not look exactly the same as it does in adulthood, but the two are related in the sense that childhood depression does make a person more at risk for adult depression; this is especially true if the childhood depression was severe.

Statistics show that there are a higher number of depressed children and teens and more of them are being seen in treatment than ever before. Is childhood depression more common today than in the past, or is it being better detected? There are more children in our population today than in previous decades, so an increase in the number of cases is understandable. In addition, improved methods of detection and increased education of professionals and the public has led to more children being diagnosed and treated for depression. However, we also know that the relative frequency is also increasing, and this means we are seeing a higher percentage of depressed children than in the past. The question we asked before, "Is childhood depression more common today than in the past, or are we just detecting it better?" can be answered, and the answer appears to be, "Yes." That is, there are relatively more cases, *and* we are detecting it better. If you review the various risk factors, many of them are more commonly found today than in the past; therefore, we should expect more cases. Certainly this is a mixed blessing. It is unsettling that there are more children who are depressed, but it is encouraging that the statistics indicate that they are being identified and treated earlier during childhood and adolescence, which gives them the chance of getting past the depression with fewer complications and problems in the future.

Treatment Issues in Children and Adolescents

The range of available treatments for mood disorders in general is discussed in later chapters, but there are several special treatment considerations for children and adolescents. The most obvious one is whether treatment is safe and effective for children. Children can react to prescription medications differently than adults, have different levels of maturity and metabolic rates, have developing bodies and nervous systems, are less sophisticated about medical/psychological issues, and as minors are legally unable to speak for themselves regarding treatment decisions. Of course most providers would discuss treatment plans with their minor patients, but the actual legal decisions about treatment lie in the hands of the responsible adults (usually the parents) in the child's life.

Similar concerns are associated with other forms of treatment. For example, medical procedures (e.g., psychosurgery) are rarely used on children—as would be expected. Children do not respond well to many forms of psychotherapy because they often lack the verbal abilities and insight to benefit from them. Consequently, it is more common to use behavioral forms of treatment, family therapy, and parental counseling when treating a child for depression; treatment needs to be appropriate for the age and developmental level of the child or youth. Treatments today are better and safer than in the past, but it is important to remain careful and vigilant about their use and appropriateness. Concerns about the safety and possible overuse of antidepressant medications with youngsters are discussed in a later chapter.

DEPRESSION IN OLDER ADULTS

Another group of citizens whose mental health needs have been neglected is the elderly, and many misconceptions about them and their treatment should be unraveled. Often it is thought that the elderly are retired and basically have it pretty easy without much to be depressed about! However, many elderly worry about finances, health issues, family matters, the nation, the world, etc., and their concerns tend to magnify and intensify over the years. The elderly often possess more risk factors for developing depression such as failing health, alienation or isolation from families and friends, the death of loved ones, moving away, living in a nursing home or adult care facility, as well as facing their own mortality. They may be living on a fixed income and are having difficulties meeting their financial needs. Being retired also means they often do not have productive outlets for their energy and creativity, and it may be difficult to feel that their lives have any meaning or importance. However, research shows that illness or other adversities are not a sufficient explanation for depression in anyone, including the elderly.

A tragic reason why older people live with depression is that they remain one of the most undertreated groups within most cultures due to short-sighted misconceptions among societies, politicians, and even medical and mental health professionals. Thus, this highly treatable condition, which produces even more difficulties for a group that is dealing with many important issues already, frequently goes unrecognized and ignored.

Symptoms of Depression in the Elderly

Many of the symptoms of depression in older adults mimic physical diseases, which makes it more difficult to identify what is depression and what is not. Although no single patient would manifest all of the possible symptoms of depression, the following list represents those found in the elderly:

- Agitation
- Anxiety
- Persistent, vague physical complaints
- Memory/concentration problems
- Social withdrawal
- Changes in appetite; weight loss or gain
- Sleep problems (insomnia, hypersomnia, fragmented sleep, and others)

- Irritability and demeaning of others
- Decreased personal care
- Confusion, delusions, hallucinations
- Feelings of discouragement and hopelessness
- Sadness, lack of playfulness, inability to laugh
- Anhedonia (lack of pleasure)
- Prolonged grief (longer than expected)
- Loss of self-worth
- Reduced energy and fatigue
- Abnormal thoughts, excessive or inappropriate guilt
- Suicidality

It might be surprising to see the more serious symptoms such as delusions and hallucinations on the list of symptoms of depression, but as mentioned earlier, some severe forms of major depressive disorder do have psychotic symptoms.

Incidence of Depression in the Elderly

The National Institute of Mental Health (NIMH) estimated that at least 1 million of the 31 million Americans over the age of 65 have major depressive disorder, and an additional 5 million have significant depressive symptoms. Although depression rates tend to decrease as adults reach their thirties, the rates begin to increase again as people live past 65 years. This indicates that when people reach their older years, risk factors increase once again, and they are more susceptible to developing depression, which may involve considering suicide as well as having increased death rates due to other medical conditions because of the depression.

Although it may be "understandable" why older people might develop depression, we must remember that, as concluded by the NIMH, being depressed is not a normal condition of aging. They suggest that depression is frequently ignored or dismissed by family, friends, and health professionals, which can lead to either untreated or undertreated symptoms occasionally resulting in suicide.

In all fairness, symptoms of depression are similar to symptoms of other diseases or conditions and are also like some normal patterns of aging (e.g., slowing down, less sleep, not as much energy). In addition, depressive symptoms are sometimes confused with the side effects of medications a person is taking. However, the NIMH stresses that when depression in the elderly is appropriately diagnosed and treated the results are usually positive, and the older patients get better and have fuller and more rewarding lives.

Specific Problems with Depression in Older Adults

One of the problems in the treatment of the elderly for all conditions is that very often bias and stereotyping can distort the picture and can lead to erroneous expectations and assumptions about them; unfortunately, these misconceptions often guide decisions about treatment. Although there may not be a diagnostic bias regarding older people and depression, research does indicate that physicians tend to be less optimistic about treatment outcomes for older people than younger patients, and especially for depression. In addition, there are also many other misconceptions about depression in the elderly. For example, women are more prone to depression when transitioning into menopause, and some people, and even health professionals, are too quick to assume that mood changes are "just hormonal—don't worry about it." Hormone changes are an inadequate and overly simplistic view of women and depression, and most women transition into menopause well before they would be considered "elderly" anyway, making the hormonal explanation irrelevant.

One factor that can interfere with an accurate diagnosis of depression in older people is that they tend to express their depressive symptoms in primarily physical rather than emotional terms. Therefore, the treating professional is likely to conclude that the described symptoms are secondary to medical conditions that should be the focus of treatment, and research suggests that most physicians will focus first and foremost on physical symptoms often to the exclusion of any emotional symptoms that are presented.

Impact of Depression on Older Adults

Depression affects the quality of life in the elderly in many ways. It can increase the impairment a person suffers from other physical medical conditions, impede improvement from other conditions, and increase the likelihood of death from physical illness. In the elderly, depression also tends to last longer than in younger patients, but psychotherapy can decrease the secondary problems and keep depression from further complicating other medical conditions. Depression does impair an elderly patient's ability to participate in the treatment of their other conditions, but this can also improve with appropriate treatment for the depression.

With these findings it is not surprising that the health care costs for older adults who suffer from depression are approximately 50 percent higher than other aged patients who are not depressed. Depressed patients rate the health care they receive as worse, visit emergency rooms more often, and in general attend more doctor appointments than their peers who are not depressed.

The elderly who are depressed also show a broad range of mental and intellectual symptoms including deficits in learning, memory, concentration/attention, perception, and mental/physical tasks. These deficits are also found when comparing depressed elderly with depressed younger adults, which means that the depressed elderly have more cognitive (mental) deficits than younger people who are also depressed. This is particularly important because some of the symptoms of depression are similar to the symptoms of dementia, also a major concern for the elderly, and therefore it is very important to accurately diagnose and appropriately treat these symptoms.

Gender Differences in Depression in the Elderly

There is also some evidence that elderly men and women experience other differences relative to depression. According to the NIMH, retired men may develop problems with depression if they have been the major wage earner for their families and still highly identify with their jobs. Retirement often leads to a sense of loss of an important role, decreased self-esteem, and additional stress resulting from numerous other losses. Further, the primary social group for men is often their employee peers, and when they retire they feel cut off from an important source of companionship and support. Men seem to experience more of the physical symptoms of depression in general, and this is also true in the elderly.

Suicide in the Elderly

One of the important issues regarding depression in the older adult population, especially for men who are widowed or divorced, is that it places them at higher risk for suicide. Even when depression is recognized in the elderly, often the risk of suicide is not considered. Some family members or friends might believe that if a person has lived a full life and they rationally decide that the pain of continuing to live is no longer worth the effort, then they should be permitted to end their life in a quiet and comfortable manner. However, as reasonable as this might sound, it must also be pointed out that suicidal ideation and the wish to be dead are often symptoms of a psychological disorder—especially depression. This suggests that, if these are symptoms of a treatable disorder, providing appropriate treatment is a more reasonable approach than helping them to commit suicide. This is a complex social, legal, and psychological issue that is beyond the scope of this book. Although physicians should try to respect a patient's needs and wishes, it would be a mistake to confuse a person's right to die with the option of dealing with a treatable condition like depression. With appropriate treatment affected individuals may begin to feel better, and there is a good chance that suicide will no longer be an attractive option. Regardless of personal feelings about "right to die" issues, the most important concern must be the accurate diagnosis and treatment of psychological conditions like depression in an effective and timely manner.

Social Factors and Depression in the Elderly

Older patients are often reluctant to discuss feelings of sadness, grief, or anhedonia with doctors because they may be embarrassed or "don't want to waste the doctor's time." Research shows that a combination of poor health and concerns about health care expenses caused some depressive symptoms in normal elderly citizens who had not been living in an institution or other care facility and had not been identified as needing treatment for depression previously. One of the biggest concerns faced by the elderly is their fear of being a burden on others. However, it is encouraging to note that by improving the quality of social support their concerns can be addressed, and this often results in the older person actually feeling better.

Self-Help Activities That Help with Depression in the Elderly

It is crucial to *listen* to patients in order to understand their needs and what is important to them. Some activities that can help depressed older adults are also beneficial for all elderly people. These include:

- Mild exercise—with doctor's approval, of course
- Music (to listen to or even participate in)
- Pets or pet visits
- Gardening or other hobbies
- Reminiscing
- Visiting others
- Good nutrition (including appropriate vitamins—with doctor's approval)
- Avoiding or only minimally using alcohol
- Learning new things (including skills)
- Volunteering to help others
- Joining and participating in a religious/spiritual community

The elderly usually appreciate the opportunity to do something meaningful and often respond gratefully and enthusiastically when given the chance to participate in something significant. Social activities and opportunities to do things with others are usually very positive additions to the lives of older adults.

Activities for Family and Friends

As mentioned above, elderly patients fear being a burden to those around them, often leading to isolation and refusals of help. It is important for family and friends to stay involved and encourage them without nagging. Activities that others can do for an elderly depressed patient include:

- Offer emotional support
- See that the depression is diagnosed and treated
- Make sure that medications are taken on time as prescribed
- Encourage treatment compliance with all aspects of treatment
- Remind the patient to stay away from alcohol, particularly if they are taking medication
- Invite the patient to participate in activities with you and be persistent (but do not "nag")
- Reassure them and comfort them
- Watch for suicidality; don't dismiss signs that are of concern to you

A challenge when dealing with persons who are depressed is they frequently behave as though they do not need or want help. They can be so discouraged and pessimistic that they feel hopeless, which is why persistent encouragement is so important. If they do not respond, do not be a pest, but drop it and then try again at another time; eventually they will probably agree to try something, even if they feel it will not make a difference. However, it is not the job of family and friends to "treat" the depression—leave that to the professionals. The depressed elderly need family and friends to be supportive and available, and they do not need someone else telling them what to do, what to take, and how to feel; just be there, listen, and be supportive.

SUMMARY

Dealing with depression in older adults is rarely easy, especially when this condition is often ignored or minimized. It is important to remember that depression in the elderly is neither inevitable nor untreatable, and the quality of a person's life and health can be dramatically improved by treating this disorder. Unfortunately, our society does not traditionally value becoming older as in cultures where the aged are venerated and supported. We often do everything we can to avoid aging, and when people get old and difficult to manage, some tend to "ship them off" or ignore them. For many, adult communities and retirement villages are places where we send the elderly in order to avoid them. However, it is encouraging to view these supportive environments as places that offer stimulation and care and allow people to live among peers who have similar needs and interests.

The age, wisdom, humor, and life experiences of those who came before us are a wealth of information that we might never have access to again, and should be treasured and savored rather than hidden, neglected, or ignored. The best way to deal with depression in the elderly is to treat them as capable adults who should be a part of society and our culture in general, and who deserve the care and treatment that is appropriate for their age and condition.

6

❖❖❖

Special Groups and Depression: Race, Ethnicity, and Sexual Orientation

INTRODUCTION

There is nothing "fair" about depression; it can affect anyone of any group and sometimes without any apparent reason. This chapter examines depression as it affects different racial and ethnic groups as well as the gay and lesbian community. Information about how depression affects special groups of people in our society has been sparse until very recently. However, we know that this disorder can appear differently within distinct groups and can be caused by different factors. Since people of minority status often face numerous and different types of risk factors, their rate of depression varies as well; in addition, however, they also share risk factors commonly found in other social and ethnic groups. For example, women of childbearing years are higher risk for depression regardless of their race, ethnicity, or culture. It is also true that certain personality traits may be related to depression across groups as well. For example, it is reported that in white, Asian, and African American college students perfectionism was a significant predictor of depression regardless of the race or ethnicity of the student.

As our country and the rest of the world become more diverse, mental health concerns become increasingly more complex and important as public health issues. It is important to note that according to the U.S.

Census Bureau the adult minority population in the United States is expected to increase from 23 percent in 2004 to 40 percent in the near future, and minority children are expected to move from 33 percent in 2004 to 48 percent as well. In 2004 67 percent of the U.S. population were white, non-Hispanic; 14 percent were Hispanic; 12 percent were African American; 5 percent were Asian/Pacific Islander; 1 percent were Native American/Alaskan Native; and 7 percent were "other." In 2003 people of Hispanic origin passed African Americans as the largest of the minority groups. The most diverse population groups in the United States are on the East and West coasts and along the border with Mexico. We are not only seeing an increase in minority populations in general but also within the minority elderly age group; in fact, Asians and Latinos are the two fastest growing groups of elderly immigrants.

CULTURAL DIFFERENCES IN DEPRESSION AND RELATED PROBLEMS

As the population becomes more culturally diverse, increased problems like prejudice and discrimination are more likely to occur. With respect to mental health issues, one of our concerns is how minority status might affect the diagnosis and treatment of mood disorders. One report found that 43 percent of African Americans and 28 percent of Latinos feel that health care professionals treat them badly because of their race and/or economic background as opposed to 5 percent of whites. A related finding is that ethnic minorities in the United States are less likely to utilize mental health services—especially Hispanics and Asians.

People from different cultures often look at and respond to mental illness differently. Their responses may indicate an unwillingness or inability to seek appropriate help, but they will also reflect the extent to which families and friends will be supportive of one who is having psychological problems. In some Asian cultures mental illness reflects badly on the family and may even interfere with one's marriage chances. Statistically, African Americans tend to be overdiagnosed with schizophrenia and underdiagnosed with bipolar disorder. They also tend to have a slower metabolism with respect to some antipsychotic and antidepressant medications, which makes them more likely to experience side effects and less likely to tolerate adequate therapeutic doses of their medications. Living in a remote location can also limit treatment opportunities, and about one-third of Native Americans or Native Alaskans do not have a doctor or a clinic where they can seek even the most basic medical and mental health treatments or reasonable preventive health care.

Suicide, always a concern in depressed persons, is also affected by racial and cultural differences. For example, the annual suicide rate is higher for males in general, but Mexican and Puerto Rican males had lower suicide rates than whites, possibly because they frequently come from predominantly Catholic cultures, and the Catholic Church views suicide as a mortal sin. Some studies find no difference in depression between whites and minorities while other studies find higher rates among minorities; clearly this is not an unambiguous situation. This fact is probably most reflective of the lack of depth and breadth of research and theory that would lead to a coherent body of knowledge in this field. Fortunately this is changing, and we are finding more and better scholarship in this area in recent years.

Depression and Social Class in Minorities

Differences in depression rates and symptoms between racial groups can be explained, at least in part, by socioeconomic status. In fact, many assert that most differences in depressive symptoms are due to socioeconomic status rather than ethnicity. It is also suggested that many of the cognitive models of depression are valid across ethnic groups, for example, feelings of low self-confidence, hopelessness, and cognitive errors that predict depression across all ethnic groups. Researchers also find that cognitive-behavioral interventions work equally well across various groups. However, we must remember that the relationship between socioeconomic status and depression is somewhat confusing and not as clear as some would like to think.

We can assume, however, that independent of social class, one's ethnic background will have some effect on the way the symptoms of depression are manifested and that ethnicity may play some part in the cause of depression. Any person with more than one risk factor has a greater likelihood of developing depression, which puts people of minority status frequently in "double jeopardy." For example, if a person is elderly and African American they have two factors that can place them at risk for various conditions—including depression. If a person is a member of a minority ethnic group, and they also happen to be female *and* elderly, they then have several risk factors working against them simultaneously. This does not, of course, guarantee that they will develop depression, but it does make them higher risk.

African Americans and Depression

For African Americans, racism, poverty, and poor health have been found to significantly infringe on their quality of life and, as we know, the lower one's quality of life the more likely one is to be a victim of depression. Since African Americans are disproportionately found to be victims of racism, poverty, and poor health, they are more likely to suffer depression. It is reported that 40 percent of all African American children are raised in poverty and that African American families earn about 60 percent of the median income in the United States, possessing only about 10 percent of the family wealth in this country. They are also more likely to pay for mental health services out of pocket, to terminate treatment prematurely, to be hospitalized for mental problems, and are frequently treated with older, less preferred medications; understandably, many African Americans do not trust the mental health system.

It is difficult to determine the exact role of race in the cause of depression, but when factors other than race are accounted for, one study reports that African Americans are less likely to suffer from major depressive disorder and dysthymic disorder than are whites; however, other studies report different results, and thus this issue has yet to be fully resolved. In one study of adolescents, it was found that even when socioeconomic status was controlled for, depression was found at higher rates among African American youths, and they assumed the differences were due to experiences of discrimination and exposure to victimization, which fits into the supposition that being higher risk is dependent upon the number of risk factors a person has. One other study found that if there was perceived or reported family conflict, this was predictive of depression in adolescent African American young women, apparently due to the indirect effect of conflict on the feelings of attachment between the child and parent.

It has also been found that mental health professionals were 60 percent more likely to diagnose a mental health problem in boys if they were black or Hispanic than if they were white, regardless of the race of the professional. Another study reported that clinicians tended to find less mental illness in blacks than whites with similar symptoms, and though this may seem to be contradictory with other research, the explanations are very compelling. Blacks were less likely to receive a mental health diagnosis and were far more likely to be judged as delinquent and referred to the juvenile justice system. Therefore, if clinicians *only* judge symptoms, they tend to see more pathology in black or Hispanic youths than in whites. However, if they are making diagnoses for the purpose of treatment, they will more likely to send black youths to the legal system and whites to the mental health system. Some have argued that blacks are less likely to benefit from treatment, but there is considerable evidence to the contrary. There is a growing body of experimental literature that supports the idea that minority groups will respond equally as well to cognitive-behavioral therapy as whites. Therefore, there is no therapeutic reason to refer blacks and other minorities to the legal system because of the mistaken belief that they might not respond to treatment.

African American males, like white males, are less likely than females to seek medical and mental health care regardless of income level. Even when treatment is free, men are less likely to seek treatment than are women. There is no evidence that there is a genetic basis for racial differences in depression, but there is good evidence that some of the social and other risk factors that are related to depression may exist to a higher degree in the black community.

Hispanics and Depression

In the United States the Hispanic population is over 36 million people, which is an increase of over 700 percent in the last 40 years. In terms of mental health issues, one-third of these 36 million people have no health insurance, half do not have a personal physician, and about 30 percent of immigrant Hispanics are depressed. We often think of Hispanics as one group, but it is actually a very heterogeneous group of people. Being of Hispanic origin can mean that they are of full or partial Hispanic heritage, they are Spanish speaking, or have immigrated from Latin America. The major subgroups of Hispanics in the United States are Mexican (60 percent of Latinos), Puerto Rican (10 percent of Latinos), and Cuban (3 percent of Latinos).

As mentioned earlier, we know less about depression and how it affects minority groups than we do about the majority white population, but this is an area where the literature is expanding and improving. Hispanic immigrants (both legal and illegal) are one minority group that receives considerable media attention and are the subject of heated debate. One study found that among immigrant Mexican Americans, mental health in general was poor with 40 percent indicating levels of anxiety and depression that might impair normal functioning. However, the basis for depression did seem to have gender relativity in this group, as it does in the white majority population, with more women than men reporting depression. In Mexican American men, social marginalization was more often associated with higher levels of depression, while stress that was related to the separation from family was more often related to depression in women. One would expect there to be differences in the salient issues regarding depression in different groups of people. In most Latino cultures the family is very important, and thus feelings of hopelessness are more likely to be related to interpersonal difficulties. Although this tendency may affect women more than men, it is still a factor that applies to both. In Latino men, higher levels of machismo and restrictions on emotions are associated with higher levels of stress and depression, a pattern that is very similar to what was found in common with non-Hispanic white men.

In any minority group, issues of discrimination often lead to feelings of personal distress and lower self-esteem, and these factors can similarly lead to depression and other mental health disorders. Unfortunately, the majority group in any population typically does not recognize "discrimination" as a potential risk factor for mental health issues like depression, which obviously compounds the problem and makes the effects more difficult to manage both personally and socially. One interesting finding is that Mexican immigrants who have lived in the United States for less than 13 years have far lower rates of depression than Mexican Americans who were born here. The most obvious interpretation of these data is that the cumulative effect of discrimination over many years is significant, but there is not yet enough evidence to prove the actual cause of this difference.

Hispanics experience mood disorders at about the same rate as whites, but this fact by itself may be misleading because we know there is inadequate treatment of depression in Hispanics, and we know that Hispanics do not have access to the quality of health care that is usually available to whites. This suggests that, even though some studies find that Hispanics and whites have about the same rate of mood disorders, we are missing many more Hispanic cases because they are less likely to attract the attention of the mental health care system due to language differences, health literacy barriers, physical presentation of depressive symptoms, and culturally different ways to express distress. Interestingly, when appropriately diagnosed, Hispanics are usually amenable to treatment for depression, often preferring psychotherapy to medication. This group seems to respond well to both types of treatment, either together or separately, which is an important reason for making sure that they are identified and treated—there is a good chance of their responding favorably to a therapeutic intervention.

As mentioned above, much of the research on depression in minority groups is very recent and presents many of the problems that all new areas of research face, such as a lack of a coherently organized and cohesive body of theory to direct and motivate research. Researchers should be congratulated for breaking ground in this important but difficult area of study because much of the literature on mental health issues in Hispanics has been plagued by problems such as weak methodology and stereotypic interpretations. However, there are still ample opportunities for research-ers and theorists to make substantial contributions in this area.

Asians and Pacific Islanders and Depression

In recent years we have seen an increase in immigration from various parts of Asia and the Pacific Islands. It is reported that 40 percent of Southeast Asian refugees are depressed, 35 percent have anxiety disor-ders, 14 percent have PTSD, and many of the Southeast Asian refugees experienced very traumatic events in their former homelands. Another troubling statistic is that the suicide rate for elderly Chinese is 10 times higher than for elderly whites. Among college students, Asian Americans score higher on measures of depression and social anxiety than do whites. In fact, depression is the most common mental health problem reported by Asians, a rate often higher than that of whites. In general, Asian Americans report higher rates of serious mental health problems than other racial and ethnic groups.

As with other minority groups, Asians are not a homogeneous group and also underuse mental health services in the United States. According to the U.S. Department of Health & Human Services only 17 percent of Asian Americans with psychological problems sought assistance and less than 6 percent did so from a mental health professional. Stigma and shame, as well as the challenge of finding services, make it difficult for Asian Americans to acknowledge problems and to follow through with obtaining appropriate services.

Treating depression in those of Asian ancestry is difficult for many of the same reasons we found with the Hispanic population. Accessing ad-equate care, agreeing to see a mental health professional, and dealing with language and/or cultural differences are all important hurdles that have to be faced. Also, people of Asian background are more likely to present with somatic symptoms of depression than other ethnic groups, which means that they are less likely to recognize the psychological basis of their problems. Professionals who treat depression psychotherapeu-tically frequently use cognitive types of strategies in order to address differing cultural concerns. Adjusting the strategy to the cultural dis-tinctions of the relevant group as well as being sensitive to the unique individual differences of the person in treatment is good practice for treating Asians or people from any other group as well. It also accentu-ates the importance of training clinicians with more awareness and knowledge of dealing with cultural differences in the context of treating psychological disorders.

DEPRESSION IN THE LESBIAN, GAY,
AND BISEXUAL COMMUNITY

Lesbian, gay, and bisexual (LGB) persons are often grouped together as a minority, and as such are often the object of discrimination and prejudice. They are, of course, a heterogeneous group that includes men and women from all racial, cultural, social, and ethnic backgrounds. Stereotyping and treating LGB persons unfairly can contribute to the multiple risk factors for depression that they are exposed to. There is a heterosexual bias in the training of mental health professionals, of which most people are not even aware. This means that the training most mental health professionals receive is only (or predominantly) focused on the heterosexual population. The majority of mental health practitioners do not have appropriate training to deal with the LGB community (or other minorities for that matter). This particular group of people might best be thought of as the hidden minority because other than their sexual orientation they are simply part of their own racial, ethnic, cultural, or subcultural group. Of course, if they are also a member of another minority, this compounds the issue of discrimination and the fears they must face, increasing the risk for mental health problems like depression.

There is evidence, similar to what is found with other minority groups, which links perceived discrimination based on sexual orientation with depression, attachment anxiety, and avoidance behaviors. Attachment anxiety is characterized by an excessive need for approval from others and a fear of interpersonal rejection or of abandonment; it is often related to the onset of depression. Other studies have demonstrated that being a gay male is not only stressful but is associated with higher levels of psychological distress, which, as we have demonstrated earlier, is related to a higher incidence of depression. Certainly, being part of an out-group can be stressful, but the additional weight of fear and discrimination can have a wide range of psychological consequences as well.

Gay and bisexual men show evidence of a higher prevalence of depression, panic attacks, and psychological distress than heterosexual men. However, lesbian and bisexual women are more prone to develop generalized anxiety disorder than heterosexual women. Interestingly, one difference between the LGB community and other minority groups is that they tend to use mental health services at a higher rate than does the majority of the heterosexual community. This, then, is one difference between the LGB community and the heterosexual community that is a positive and encouraging trend.

One subgroup of the LGB community that is less visible and often outside of the range of accessible help is LGB youth; they often have to deal with either living a completely secret life or risking total rejection as well as conflict with family and friends. Gay youth are the only group of adolescents who often face total rejection from their families with little prospect of ongoing support. Obviously, these youths belong to two very high risk groups—being young and also being homosexual; people who have these two characteristics are 2–3 times more likely to attempt suicide than other young people. In fact, it is estimated that they may comprise up to 30 percent of completed suicides annually. When we are able to determine the motives behind these suicides, they often seem to involve the discrepancies with which the gay youth must live continually. They must face discrimination, humiliation, rejection, and abandonment, or they can live a life of lies, deception, emptiness, and emotional isolation. A majority of homosexual suicide attempts occur before age 20 and nearly one-third occur before the age of 17.

With respect to the adult segment of the LGB community, about 25 percent of lesbians and 20 percent of gay men have attempted suicide. In fact, gay males are six times more likely to attempt suicide than are heterosexual males, and lesbian women are twice as likely to attempt suicide as heterosexual women. Another study found that when people were questioned as to whether they had ever attempted or *contemplated* suicide, 40 percent of gay males and 39 percent of lesbian women affirmed that they had.

One fact that seems surprising, given the stress and discrimination that LGB people face daily, is that the rate of psychological problems in this community is not higher. In fact, some studies do not find many differences in depression rates between LGB people and heterosexuals. Some studies report that gay men are less defensive and less self-confident than heterosexual men, while lesbian women are more self-confident than heterosexual women. They also found no difference in personal adjustment between the homosexual and heterosexual groups. Although this is at odds with other studies, it does suggest that being gay or lesbian does not necessarily mean they experience higher levels of psychological disorders.

A study that looked at Latino lesbian women and gay men reported that although certainly at risk for depression, they showed resilience through coping, high self-esteem, and relatively low levels of depression. It also reported that people who perceived more social support experienced less depression. This is a finding that is consistent with other studies of gay men as well as studies on heterosexual men. Aspects of collective self-esteem were also related to lower levels of psychological abnormality, an important finding that demonstrates that collective positive self-esteem can directly affect depression rates within the Latino LGB community in a positive direction—that is, it helps.

An ethical issue associated with treating LGB clients is that a therapist must be aware of any negative biases they may harbor about this client group and deal with it through diversity training, personal counseling, continuing education courses, more supervision with this type of client, etc. A therapist may feel that they should try to convert the LGB client to a "normal" lifestyle and may argue that the LGB lifestyle is so stressful and demeaning that changing the sexual orientation of the client is really in the client's best interest. However, unless the client brings this topic up and requests such a change, the therapist should never presume to dictate the agenda for therapy just because it fits with the therapist's values. So-called conversion therapy has never been very successful and is considered unethical by most mental health professionals. In fact, the only way that it wouldn't be considered unethical is if the client introduces the topic themselves and asks to set this as a goal in therapy. It is vitally important that a therapist find ways to affirm the client before sexual orientation is disclosed or becomes an issue in treatment. A therapist must do this with all clients, but it is of the utmost importance if the client is from a group that is typically marginalized by society and the health care system.

SUMMARY AND CONCLUSIONS

As you can see, the more we learn about depression, the more complicated it becomes, especially when cultural differences are introduced into the equation. While certain risk factors may be more applicable to one group or another, we do know that the more risk factors that are present, the more likely a person is to suffer from depression. It has also been demonstrated that acceptable treatments seem to work for most groups regardless of age, race, ethnicity, gender, or sexual orientation. We have found, however, that treatment by a professional who is unfamiliar with a particular group's culture may be problematic and most certainly wouldn't be as effective. Although people of a minority group are usually not as likely to seek and receive treatment, the LGB group of clients seems to go against this general trend.

Regardless of a patient's origin and culture, each client deserves the respect of the treating professional. If a professional is uncomfortable with the values of a particular client, and it is creating a problem in treatment, the professional must refer the client to a different provider who is experienced and comfortable with the issues being addressed. Most clinical settings deal with a more diverse client population today than ever before, and therefore this is a more common issue in treatment today. Mental health professionals need to think about diversity within their practice, institutional and educational settings, and in their research. To the extent that we are educated and sensitive to culture, race, gender, age, and lifestyle differences, we will be better able to address these issues in treatment. There are many books, articles, training programs, and workshops available to increase one's knowledge and skills—the best professionals take advantage of these opportunities.

7

❖❖❖

Treatment of Depression: Psychological Therapies

INTRODUCTION

This chapter deals with some of the different types of psychological treatments for depression. The basis of the psychological approach is that a flawed psychological process leads to a disorder of mood—in this case, depression. The question, "Is depression a biological or psychological problem?" can only be answered, "Yes." A biological dysfunction can produce psychological symptoms, but the underlying biology should never be the only focus for trying to understand something as complex as depression. The psychological aspects are ultimately where we need to try to comprehend the nature and impact of this disorder.

It is important to remember that psychological problems that have a social or interpersonal cause can lead to biological changes in the central nervous system and to other parts of the body. Therefore, while it is true that biological factors can produce depressive symptoms, it is also true that disorders like depression can also cause changes in biological systems. While medications can often be very helpful in the treatment of the biological aspects of depression, it is clear that psychological treatments are even more important to fully recover from depression. Psychologists consider three primary factors when developing treatment approaches: thoughts, feelings, and behaviors (although there are other factors that are important as well). Each psychotherapeutic approach is formulated and structured in a manner that addresses therapeutic change within one, two, or all three of these areas—thoughts, feelings, and behaviors. The basic idea in therapeutic change is to help people make changes that will positively affect their lives and help them to be happier, more content, and optimally functional in all of the important areas of their lives.

EARLY HISTORY OF PSYCHOTHERAPY

Psychotherapy is a relatively recent tool in the mental health therapies. Historically, we have seen many different, sometimes bizarre, and often horrific types of therapies used to treat the mentally ill. Since many of the early thinkers assumed that faulty biology was at the base of mental illness, most of the early treatments were biological. Some evidence was discovered in prehistoric humans that suggests a type of brain surgery where a hole was cut in the skull as a form of treatment; this is called "trephining." It is assumed this surgery was intended to "fix" a problem in the brain, or perhaps release a troublesome "spirit." Since some of the skulls of patients (or victims) of this treatment had calcified edges on the holes in the skull, it is obvious that the "patient" survived the treatment long enough for the cut bone edges to calcify.

Over the millennia people have conceptualized and treated mental illness in many different ways. The early Greeks were inclined to treat the mentally ill with kindness and support, but as history entered into the Middle Ages the treatments became much harsher and less supportive. While we don't know as much about history in other parts of the world, we do know that in Europe during the Middle Ages official judgment about mental illness was generally governed by the Catholic Church. Typically, it was assumed that if someone was behaving in a "crazy" manner they were possessed by demons, in league with the devil, or were inflicted by a mental disease as punishment for some type of sin. Thus, the treatment was generally vicious and often fatal. If one was possessed, the host body had to be rendered so unpleasant that the invading demon would leave to find a more hospitable home. If the person was in league with the devil or was being tormented because of sin, they were "obviously deserving" of severe punishment. In the name of treatment, people were tortured, maimed, and even killed.

At least in Europe it wasn't until the Renaissance and the Age of Enlightenment that attitudes and treatment of the mentally ill began to change. Philipe Pinel and others started to "unchain the insane" and to treat them kindly and supportively. Some called the new approach to treatment "moral therapy," but it was really just kind and supportive care. Any true therapeutic gains were probably based primarily on the patient themselves; within a kinder and more helpful environment this would have been easier to accomplish. Eventually, mental illness was removed from the religious realm and returned to the medical sphere, which led primarily to biological treatments including bleeding, some medications (not very effective ones by today's standards), and other treatments such as convulsive therapy (performed with electricity or drugs), physical restraint, nutrition, hydrotherapy (strapping patients in warm baths for hours), psychosurgery (lobotomies where incisions were made in the brain to separate part of the frontal lobes from other areas of the brain), and other therapies that are strange by today's standards.

These types of approaches were popular until Freud came along and began to postulate purely psychological mechanisms for understanding human personality and pathology. However, even Freud, whose training was as a physician and physiologist, suggested that there were biological factors underlying all psychological processes. He did state that the psychic energy system was derived from the biological energy system but became independent of it and was parallel to it throughout a person's life. From this time forward, we have seen the growth of psychological theories about the human psyche and the abnormal processes that might emerge from it.

Freud was exposed to the exploration of the "functional" (nonmedical) aspects of mental pathology when he studied with the French psychopathologists Charcot, Janet, and Liebeault. They were trying to understand the psychological aspects of what was then called "hysteria" but today is known as conversion disorder. This interesting disorder is manifested as a physical symptom but without any underlying physical illness. In addition, the French psychopathologists were the first to discover that hypnosis actually produced temporary relief from the symptoms of hysteria. His work led Freud back to Vienna where he worked under the supervision of Josef Breuer in order to become a consulting neurologist. In fact, it was Breuer who discovered the "talking cure" for hysteria when he found that, even without using hypnosis, hysteric patients experienced temporary relief from their symptoms by simply talking about them and about themselves and events in their lives. Freud learned from Breuer and credited him with his early discoveries. From this beginning Freud undertook the enormous task of developing a purely psychological theory of human personality and psychopathology (abnormal psychology), which developed into a new way of understanding and treating mental illness—psychoanalysis.

PSYCHOLOGICAL TREATMENTS FOR DEPRESSION

There are literally hundreds of different approaches to psychotherapy for depression, but most of them fall into one of the following groups: psychodynamic, humanistic/existential, cognitive and cognitive/behavioral, the purely behavioral, and family and/or group methods. Each of these approaches deals with the treatment of depression, and there are similarities and differences among them.

Psychodynamic

The psychodynamic approaches generally assume that depression results from an event (or events) in the past that is often related to loss. It is challenging for a person to deal with this loss because the real, imagined, or symbolic loss is often buried in the subconscious. The more traditional types of psychodynamic therapies (e.g., psychoanalysis) try to uncover the subconscious root of the problem, bring it to conscious awareness, and then work to resolve the original conflict, thus relieving the patient of their symptoms.

Some of the newer psychodynamic approaches work more directly with information from a person's present daily life and relationships, but the logic is much the same—an underlying problem must be identified. The person must find ways to deal with this and similar issues so that the same problems do not keep re-emerging. Unlike the spectacular cures often found in the media, the "cure" is never as simple as an insight that leads to an "Ah-ha!" experience that suddenly changes a person into a fully integrated and healthy individual; this makes for good a movie, but it is never that simple.

The research literature has not been very supportive of psychodynamic therapy as a treatment for depression; however, this form of treatment works very well with some patients who prefer this approach. The longer-term psychoanalytic types of therapy have only *occasionally* been found to be helpful in the treatment of unipolar depression, but it is the shorter-term therapies that are most frequently supported in the empirical literature. In response to these findings, some professionals in the psychodynamic camp have begun developing and working with more time-limited and directive forms of treatment, hoping to improve the efficiency and effectiveness of this form of therapy.

At this time, the conclusion is that psychodynamic therapy is important historically, but it has not fared as well in the research literature as some of the newer, more directive forms of treatment. Although many professionals would accept the basic ideas behind the psychodynamic approach to therapy, the majority seem to feel that the newer forms of therapy are a more efficient and effective way to accomplish psychotherapeutic change.

Humanistic/Existential Therapies

During the mid- to late 1960s American society was in the midst of dramatic and sweeping social changes. The United States was reeling from post–World War II economic success and growth, and the Baby Boomer generation was coming into its own. Social issues like racial and gender equality were front-page concerns, and every town and city in America was challenged to adapt to the new ways of thinking about and treating one another. At the same time, the birth control pill became widely available, and the pre-AIDS sexual liberation era coupled with women's liberation opened up an entirely new standard of sexual freedom and expression. This was also the era of the emergence and greater acceptance of recreational drug use; it was the generation of "sex, drugs, and rock 'n roll."

In addition to these social changes, the Vietnam War, one of the most controversial and least supported of America's military adventures, became the first war to have daily television coverage, creating strong and often conflicting feelings in most people depending upon their generation and political inclinations. There was considerable political and social unrest in the United States and much of the Western world, and citizens—especially younger people—were demanding changes and improvements in society. They were beginning to think and act differently than their parents' and grandparents' generations.

Psychology was certainly not immune to these social pressures, and it began to adapt to these influences as well. Some in psychology jumped on the political and social bandwagon, and most college campuses were hotbeds of political and social unrest. A few psychologists became deeply involved with the recreational drug movement and encouraged the use of drugs as a way of expanding and enriching one's consciousness. As many younger people began to challenge the status quo and the "power elite" and were calling into question some of the basic assumptions that had been accepted as American "truths," psychology began to look at its traditional methods and assumptions and to question some of the values that American psychology seemed to accept as fundamental.

Where strict determinism was basic to the psychodynamic and behavioristic approaches to psychology, many American psychologists were challenging the premise and legitimacy of the deterministic approaches of mainstream psychology. Interestingly, they began to borrow ideas from more philosophical approaches to examining behavior. Drawing from fields in philosophy such as existentialism, humanism, and phenomenology, this "new psychology" began to grow and found many supporters among students, the public, and professional psychologists and psychiatrists as well.

Some influential and important American psychologists became involved with this new movement, including Carl Rogers, who developed a totally new approach to personality and psychotherapy based on the "self" as an experiencing, rational, feeling entity. Abraham Maslow contributed a completely new way of conceptualizing human motivation, as well as the idea that people could be and were often motivated by the highest of human values. He felt that we needed to stop focusing only on illness and examine the very best that humans could be—those he called "self-actualizers." Interestingly, both Rogers and Maslow were important as innovators, teachers, researchers, and leaders. In fact, both were elected president of the American Psychological Association during this era.

A psychiatrist who was influential during this time was Fritz Perls, who was considered the father of Gestalt psychology. This approach was in opposition to traditional American psychology and focused on a person's ability to integrate their experiences into a coherent sense of themselves, much as Rogers had. Another important contributor of this era was Rollo May, who applied existentialism to an understanding of psychology, presenting his ideas in a manner that was accessible to an educated lay public and which led to a broader acceptance of his ideas among psychologists and others. As a group, these approaches tended to be more positive, less interested in systematic research, less concerned with determinism, and more concerned with health, growth, and the importance and uniqueness of the individual.

Psychotherapies during this era all tended to reject the deterministic, therapist-guided approaches of the psychoanalysts and the behaviorists. Individual rationality, personal growth, and integration were the important bases for therapy. As psychoanalysts tended to view human nature as being guided and determined by sexual and aggressive impulses, which were largely subconscious, they saw human nature as basically negative. The behaviorists, on the other hand, looked at human nature as a tabula rasa (blank tablet) upon which experience would write its messages. Thus, for them human nature is neutral. For most of those in the humanistic and existential camps human nature is largely positive and healthy. These therapists then try to find ways to unlock and release the healthy things inside a person and to help them flourish; therapy tends to be very non-directive and client-centered. Many of these thinkers even resisted the idea that the people they were serving were "patients," and in fact, Rogers approach was called "client-centered therapy."

As influential and important as the humanistic and existential approaches have been, there is not much empirical evidence that they have been very helpful in treating mood disorders. There is probably a specific type of patient who is likely to benefit from these approaches, but that does not include the majority of patients. However, many of the practitioners of these approaches disagree with the idea that the only therapies of value are those that can be validated by empirical research. It is their position that truth can be sought and found in ways other than the scientific method, and they reject the idea that they need to prove their approach *experimentally* when they know *experientially* that what they do is of value to their clients. These approaches are not as widely utilized today as they were in recent decades, but there are still practitioners who use these types of therapy with reportedly good results. More accurately, it can be assumed that there are many therapists who integrate some of the approaches to therapy from this background along with the more conventional therapies in order to take advantage of both perspectives.

Cognitive and Cognitive/Behavioral Approaches

For many decades, psychoanalysis and some of the newer psychodynamic approaches were the primary methods for psychotherapeutic interventions. There were behaviorally oriented practitioners who were looking at ways to apply behavioristic models to psychotherapeutic processes, but most of these clinicians were in the academic realm and many of the interventions were found in the applied research literature. Consequently, most of the people who were "in the trenches" practicing psychotherapy were from the psychodynamic background.

A few people had moved away from this psychodynamic heritage but had not embraced the behavioral model and were trying to find alternative ways to conceptualize and treat abnormal behavior. The three primary sources of data for therapists are thoughts, feelings, and behaviors, and the one area that they had not utilized much in the past was the cognitive realm—dealing with people's thoughts and ideas. Some theorists and practitioners began dealing with cognitive models and, while they aroused some notice, they did not have a major impact in the field for many years. Some of the real innovators drew from earlier "rebels" in the psychoanalytic realm and introduced a new way of conceptualizing mental illness and psychotherapeutic change. From a traditional back-ground one psychoanalytically trained therapist, Albert Ellis, developed an approach he called rational/emotive psychotherapy, which looked at how faulty beliefs could lead to disordered thinking and abnormal behavior and then at how therapeutic change could result from altering these pathological belief systems.

Another of the early leaders in the cognitive field was Aaron Beck, a traditionally trained psychiatrist who focused on the dysfunctional thought patterns associated with depression and on how the treatment of depression needed to focus on these thoughts. This was particularly interesting since depression is considered to be a disorder of mood and yet, Beck felt that the best way to understand and treat depression was to focus on the thought patterns associated with it.

As the cognitive approach gained ground it became clearer that this approach would be more applicable and more powerful if coordinated with behavioral interventions, and this is when the cognitive-behavioral approach started to emerge. The next generation of psychologists worked in an environment that challenged the traditional psychoanalytic approaches. They wanted a more broadly applicable approach rather than the strictly behavioral types of interventions and began to integrate the different ideas that were now available—starting a whole new movement. Albert Bandura's work on social learning theory set the stage for much of what was to follow. Having a behaviorally based approach that also focused on thinking and perception was controversial but very compelling. Others started to develop these ideas, and they began to gain ground. Beck's work on the cognitive elements of depression started to broaden and to incorporate some of the behavioral approaches in his formulation of what depression involves. In fact, one innovative psychologist, Martin Seligman, applied his work on learned helplessness to an understanding of depression. He quickly realized, however, that this simple concept was not enough to deal with the complexity of depression, and he began to study under and collaborate with Aaron Beck. What emerged from all of this work and collaboration was a cognitive *and* behavioral approach to understanding depression.

Today, cognitive-behavioral therapy (CBT) is the most widely accepted of the psychological forms of treatment for depression, and there is substantial literature supporting its effectiveness and efficiency. Some have demonstrated that CBT results in a faster recovery from depression than other treatments, and that cognitive factors are more important in understanding depression than other personal or psychosocial factors. Historically, medication has always been the first line of treatment for depression, and it was thought that medication would produce better and quicker results than psychotherapy; however, much of the recent literature reports that cognitive/behavioral approaches produce fairly quick results. Others also found that patients who had been treated with CBT were less likely to relapse than patients who were treated with just medication. Another recent comprehensive study demonstrated that CBT works as well as medication in patients with moderate to severe depression. However, the most important finding of this study was that the CBT had long-lasting results. The patients who were treated with CBT were no more likely to relapse than those who were *still* being treated with medication. However, those treated with medication alone had significantly higher relapse rates than the therapy-alone group when the medication was discontinued.

It is clear that either CBT alone or CBT with antidepressant medications is considered to be the first-line treatment for depression; however, it is not the *only* way to successfully treat depression. Some patients prefer or are more likely to respond to other forms of treatment, and there are skilled practitioners who use other techniques effectively and successfully.

Neobehavioral Approaches to Treating Depression

As soon as cognitive therapies and behavioral treatments were joined together it seemed they were inextricably and forever linked in the minds of most psychologists. However, there remained a small group who felt that the purely behavioral approaches had been abandoned too abruptly and deserved more consideration and study. Some have pointed out that in the last quarter of the 20th century the cognitive approaches gained such strength that behavioral therapies were considered inadequate by themselves. Further, some were not so sure that the cognitive approaches were even necessary and questioned how and even if they worked as advertised. In fact, there are some behavioral practitioners and researchers who feel that the behavioral part of CBT is the main reason these approaches work so well. A number of important researchers and practitioners have expanded the realm of behavioral techniques and have developed some approaches that have shown considerable promise.

The newer behavioral therapies tend to be very technique-oriented and are based on a philosophical approach that is grounded in behavioristic theories and empirical research. No specific approach will work equally with every type of problem, but it is clear that the behavioral approach has survived many fads and keeps re-emerging with new ideas and supportive research.

OTHER PSYCHOLOGICAL APPROACHES TO TREATMENT

Interpersonal Psychotherapy (IPT)

This influential approach has demonstrated success rates close to CBT and incorporates four different types of events that may lead to depression:

- Interpersonal loss
- Interpersonal role dispute
- Interpersonal role transition
- Interpersonal defeats

Clearly, this approach is grounded in the belief that depression is linked to interpersonal difficulties, the implication being that treatment must address interpersonal issues if the depression is to be treated effectively. While not as widely used or accepted as CBT, interpersonal psychotherapy is proving to be a credible and empirically supported approach that is gaining adherents in the clinical realm, clinical research, and is often included in clinical training programs.

Couple's Therapy

It is not uncommon for troubled relationships to lead to or complicate depression. Research demonstrates that recovery from depression is often slower for people who do not receive support from their spouse or significant other. An advantage of couple's therapy is that it can be used in addition to any of the individual therapy approaches ranging from behavioral to psychodynamic. Some research has demonstrated that couples therapy can be as effective as IPT, individual therapy, or medication in the treatment of depression, but it is difficult to evaluate. It not only relies on two people as therapy clients, but either or both clients may also be involved with individual treatment, which is another factor that makes it hard to evaluate couple's therapy on its own.

Attachment-based Family Therapy (ABFT)

This approach to therapy emerged from research that demonstrated that adolescent African American females often experienced depression when there was conflict in the family and the attachment with parents was disrupted. ABFT works with the entire family (or at least the parents and targeted adolescent patient) focusing on the troubled family dynamics in order to help the adolescent deal with depression. Some research has found that ABFT is effective in reducing anxiety, depression, and family conflict for depressed adolescents; however, there is not yet enough credible research to make this assertion. One study that compares more general family therapy with CBT and supportive therapy found that in the treatment of major depressive disorder, cognitive behavioral therapy was significantly more effective than either family or supportive therapy. This does not mean that family-based therapies should not be used, but that we must determine which patient groups and problems are best served by family types of therapy.

Group Therapy

It is somewhat misleading to identify group therapy as a singular form of treatment for depression because it may involve any type of approach from psychodynamic to behavioral to cognitive to humanistic/existential, etc. Thus, coming from any background a therapist can conduct treatment with groups of patients. Some groups will focus on one type of problem (e.g., depression) while others will include people with many different types of disorders. Group therapy was much more widely used in the 1960s and 1970s and is still used to some extent today. It is logistically more difficult to administer and is difficult to evaluate because it involves many different people and may accompany other forms of treatment at the same time. Much of the research has been less than supportive of group therapy as a primary treatment approach for depression, but some have found it to be helpful in addition to medication and/or individual therapy. Group therapy has been particularly helpful in dealing with specific topic areas like grief and certain medical issues like breast cancer and cardiovascular disease.

SUMMARY AND CONCLUSIONS

One basic assumption about all of the psychological forms of treatment for depression is that, as a predominantly psychological/emotional disorder, the most appropriate form of treatment should be psychological. In the past there was considerable debate over the relationship between treatment and causality. Even today we see ads for antidepressant medications on TV stating that depression is a "medical illness" that is treated with medication. Of course, this advertisement has nothing to do with the realities of depression and has everything to do with drug companies trying to sell their products. Some people used to argue that since depression can be treated with medication, it must be a biological illness; conversely, others argued that if depression can be treated psychologically, it must be a purely psychological phenomenon. Researchers were making the erroneous assumption that an effective type of treatment was all the evidence they needed to support the causes implied by that theory. Depression is caused by many factors and is never a simple condition. There are many different forms of treatment for depression, and clinically it is most important that the therapist is concerned with treating the condition effectively *regardless* of the cause.

Most practitioners today are comfortable with the fact that there are different types of treatments available, and the job of the practitioner is to match an effective treatment with the patient and his or her needs. If one treatment doesn't seem to work very well, then try another, but make sure the patient stays with a treatment long enough to experience some results or to determine that it is not going to work. One of the most common causes of failed treatment, either medical or psychological, is when it is discontinued prematurely.

Looking at the research literature one is tempted to assume that every therapist should use CBT, a very successful and effective treatment for depression. However, in the hands of experienced and competent therapists very good results have been demonstrated with all of the types of therapy that we have discussed. For a patient to find a practitioner with whom they are comfortable, and who is well-trained, appropriately credentialed, experienced, and competent, and then to also feel that the treatment approach is reasonable and comfortable provides a very good foundation upon which to build an effective course of treatment. Good treatment results depend upon an effective treatment team, the primary team members being the patient and the treating professional; this is true regardless of the type of therapy that is practiced.

8

❖❖❖

Treatment for Depression: Medical and Alternative Methods

Men and women have suffered from depression and have attempted to find answers and remedies to cure it since the beginning of our existence. Historically, mental illness has been viewed as a moral failing, characterological weakness, evil, malingering (faking), and other typically negative explanations. Depending upon the time period and the prevailing culture, treatment was relegated to the legal system, the church, the family, and finally, to medicine. Fields such as psychology and psychiatry were not even relevant until the late 19th century, and in the absence of reasonable and effective treatments, the mentally ill, including those with depression, were treated (or not) based upon the prevailing views and theories in society at large.

When treatment gravitated into the medical sphere it is hardly surprising that the tendency was to seek medical answers and to pursue medical treatments. The search for effective medicines has always been at the forefront of treatment initiatives, but there have also been efforts to find surgeries and other physical forms of treatment that might be helpful in the treatment of depression. Medication has been and still is the most frequent form of medical treatment for any type of depression.

MEDICINE, THE BRAIN, AND DEPRESSION

In recent decades drug companies have been permitted to advertise medications, targeting their ads to the general public—including the antidepressant drugs. This approach to selling drugs offers unfortunate and misleading expectations about the nature of depression and its treatment. Prior to the 1950s there were not very many medical treatment options for depression: psychosurgery, which had proven to be dangerous and ineffective, electroconvulsive therapy (ECT), which was at that time somewhat effective but dangerous and frightening for patients, and finally, medications, which were not very effective.

The Early Antidepressants

In the 1950s some "accidental" findings ushered in two new classes of drugs that provided not only effective treatment for depression but the hope that we were finally starting to understand the underlying physiology of depression. With no apparent notion of what might happen, physicians noticed that iponiazid, a drug that was being tested on patients with tuberculosis, seemed to make patients feel happier. With further testing they found that this same effect could be observed in depressed patients. Research demonstrated that this class of drugs called monoamine oxidase inhibitors (MAOI) improved the mood and decreased the symptoms of depressed patients. They also found that this type of drug apparently worked by preventing the breakdown of some of the "chemical messengers" (neurotransmitters) that carry messages between brain cells and that were clearly related to depression. Research demonstrated that at least 50 percent of depressed patients showed improvement with the use of MAOIs.

Unfortunately, it was also discovered that the MAOIs have some serious side effects, particularly when people eat or drink certain foods or beverages. These drugs are effective, and for patients who have not responded well to conventional antidepressant medications, they can still be a valuable treatment alternative—as long as they are used carefully. In fact, a new approach using a skin patch for an MAOI has been shown to be safe without dietary restrictions at low doses.

Another class of medications was also "accidentally" discovered to be helpful for depression in the 1950s. Researchers were studying the effects of a drug called imipramine on schizophrenia. They found that it had little effect on schizophrenia, but it seemed to help unipolar depression. This drug and related compounds became known as tricyclics due to their chemical structure; they have proven to be effective in about 60–65 percent of depressed patients. It was also found that when patients discontinue a tricyclic drug too soon, they often relapse. Thus, many physicians keep their patients on these drugs indefinitely. Another complication is that the tricyclic drugs rarely reach therapeutic effectiveness in less than a few weeks, and sometimes it takes more than a month. While these drugs are certainly safer to use than the MAOIs, they are not without side effects, and some of the side effects make the drugs difficult to use with some patients (e.g., heart rhythm irregularities, dizziness, agitation, dry mouth, constipation, occasional weight gain, etc.).

The tricyclics do have some unpleasant side effects and can be lethal in overdose. In recent years, with the introduction of new antidepressant medications with fewer side effects, the tricyclics have not been used as often. However, tricyclics are being used in lower doses for chronic pain disorders, fibromyalgia, and insomnia, particularly if they have insomnia that is related to pain. Finally, some people with migraines find that taking tricyclic medication helps to decrease the frequency of headaches. While these drugs are not used as often for depression, they are still used as a second-line treatment when a patient is either treatment resistant to the newer medications or cannot tolerate the newer medications due to side effects. A related class of drugs called tetracyclics (a four-ring molecular structure) has similar advantages and disadvantages as the tricyclics and often with side effects that create problems (e.g., significant weight gain). However, for some patients these drugs work very well without significant side effect problems.

Second-Generation Antidepressants

In addition to the tetracyclics there has been an influx of newer antidepressants for the treatment of depression and anxiety disorders. The first of these drugs to create a stir (and resultant controversy) was Prozac (fluoxetine), which appeared on the market in the United States around 1987. What made this drug different was the fact that it worked *only* on serotonin, which is a neurotransmitter that is important in depression. By making more serotonin available within the brain, depressive symptoms improve for most patients. Prozac and other drugs like it are called selective serotonin reuptake inhibitors (SSRIs) since they only work on the serotonin system. While Prozac was the first drug in this category to be widely recognized, it was not the first SSRI to be developed. In fact, three other drugs were actually marketed before Prozac, but two were removed from the market because of side effects and one other named Luvox (fluvoxamine) is still on the market.

Prozac and the other SSRIs were quickly and aggressively marketed, became very popular, and were probably overused. They are not as dangerous as other antidepressants when overdosed, do not have the same troubling side effects as the tricyclics, and do not have the dietary restrictions of the MAOIs; however, that is not to say they are perfect. It takes two to six weeks for full effect, and they produce their own side effect problems. Most commonly, people taking these medications complain of nausea, digestive problems, headache, light-headedness, sexual dysfunction, and other, usually mild, difficulties. Many side effects disappear in a few days, and the ones that don't can often be eliminated by simply changing to a different medication. Because they are effective, relatively safe, easy to use, and available, these drugs are used widely and enthusiastically. The introduction of the SSRIs dramatically changed the treatment of depression and related conditions.

One class of drugs that works on two different neurotransmitters (serotonin and norepinephrine) is called the serotonin and norepinephrine reuptake inhibitors. This class of drugs deals with a broader array of neurophysiological systems and seems to work differently in treating problems in addition to depression. Each has found a specialized niche for the treatment of other conditions in addition to depression. For example, one of these drugs (Cymbalta) is used to treat pain in some patients, another is used to treat insomnia (Trazodone), and another is often used with anxiety and depression when they occur together (Effexor). The final class of the newer antidepressants is the dopamine reuptake inhibitors (DRIs). These medications block the reabsorption of dopamine (another neurotransmitter) in the central nervous system, making more of it available to carry messages between brain cells. For people who are treatment resistant to SSRIs, DRIs are often good second-line drugs. In fact, since they work differently than SSRIs they are sometimes used in combination with an SSRI, often with good results. The main drug in this category is Wellbutrin (bupropion). It is sometimes used because of the low frequency of sexual side effects and fewer problems with weight gain, both of which often lead patients to discontinue other antidepressant medication treatment. Bupropion is the same medication in the drug Zyban, which is used to help people stop smoking.

In addition to antidepressant medications, occasionally prescribers will use one of the tranquilizer drugs with a depressed patient who is also anxious. The antidepressant medications may help with anxiety but are usually slow to take effect. Since tranquilizers tend to work very quickly, they are often used at the beginning of antidepressant treatment until the slower-acting drug begins to take effect. The tranquilizer types of drugs, while effective, also have troubling side effects like the development of drug tolerance and addiction. As such, they are not used for longer-term treatment unless nothing else has proven effective for managing the anxiety symptoms.

Drug Treatment for Bipolar Disorder

While one of the characteristics of bipolar disorder (BPD) is depression, it is not as easily treated as unipolar depression since BPD involves either mania or hypomania, which are conditions not treated with antidepressant medications. The use of some antidepressants (e.g., SSRIs) in a depressed patient with BPD may actually trigger a manic episode, and prescribers must be careful when dealing with bipolar patients because there are other drugs that can cause a manic or hypomanic episode to occur. Thus, in BPD the typical strategy is to stabilize the manic or hypomanic condition first and then to treat the depression.

There are basically three classes of drugs that are used to treat manic/hypomanic conditions in bipolar patients. One class of drugs, the mood stabilizers, reduces the excitement and agitation of the manic or hypomanic patient and stabilizes them emotionally. Second, some anticonvulsant medications that are used to treat epilepsy and related conditions also have a mood-stabilizing effect. Finally, some of the newer antipsychotic medications are used to stabilize the bipolar patient who is in a manic state. These drugs are frequently used to treat conditions like schizophrenia but are sometimes helpful in treating mania/hypomania and major depressive disorder as well. The newer drugs in this category are used more often than the older ones because they have a better side effect profile, particularly with respect to the more serious side effects. However, they are not without their own concerns. Nevertheless, even these drugs can be used safely under the careful supervision of a physician (usually a psychiatrist) who will use blood tests to make sure that the medication is not creating other problems.

ANTIDEPRESSANT MEDICATIONS AND SUICIDALITY

One of the concerns that has been an issue since the beginning of the use of antidepressant medications is whether the medication itself increases suicidal risk. This is a tricky issue to study since depressed patients are already higher risk for suicide than someone who is not depressed. However, since antidepressant medications take weeks or sometimes even months to work, it is not clear that patients are at higher risk because they are on the medication or because they are still depressed and the medicine isn't working yet. While the evidence surrounding this issue is conflicted and has not led to consistent and accepted conclusions, it is clear that suicide rates have decreased since the newer antidepressants have been introduced. Due to continuing concerns, however, the Food and Drug Administration (FDA) has placed warnings on antidepressant medications regarding the possibility that a person might be more prone to suicide after starting the medication and should be monitored closely; this is especially true for children, teens, and young adults. However, it is important to note that studies indicate that the real risk for suicide is the depression more than the medication. Of course, patient welfare and safety is always the primary concern in any treatment, so closely monitoring a depressed patient is considered appropriate care under any circumstances, particularly if they are on medication; the greater risk is to not treat someone when effective treatment is available.

The research findings show that no scientific evidence causally links the newer antidepressants to increased suicide rates. The caution, however, is understandable, and it certainly is better to be careful than to have a tragic result. However, we must be mindful of the fact that there are people young and old who could benefit from treatment but who are not receiving it because of a misplaced fear of increased risk of suicide. One thing to consider is that we forget that increased suicidality typically involves conflicts that medications aren't going to fix but that psychotherapy might help. This is especially true of adolescents; good psychotherapy can be used to teach people the skills that will help them deal with life outside of therapy in such a way as to reduce their own suicidal risk—this is difficult to do with medication alone.

SUMMARY OF FINDINGS ON MEDICATIONS

While the medications that have emerged since the 1950s have proven their effectiveness in clinical practice and in the research literature, there are various reasons for using one medication over another. For example, no two patients are the same; what works for one person may not work for another, and it is difficult to predict which medication will work for a specific patient. Conventional wisdom dictates that the *main* reason medication is not initially effective is that the drug is either not prescribed at a high enough dosage or is not continued long enough. All of these medications take weeks to work, and sometimes the adjustment of the dosage may take several months to reach the correct level; often people change or stop medication before they have given the drug a chance to work.

In recent years SSRIs have usually been the first line of medication treatment; they tend to produce milder side effects than other types of antidepressants and are a lower risk for fatal overdoses and heart rhythm disturbances that can be dangerous for people with cardiac disease. Research has demonstrated that SSRIs are at least as effective as tricyclics and since they are safer and less problematic, they are usually used first.

This does not mean that medication is the only or even necessarily the best form of treatment. As we learned earlier, medication alone as the treatment for depression frequently results in relapse when the drug is stopped. None of the medications are without side effects, and this always has to be balanced with therapeutic advantages.

OTHER MEDICAL TREATMENTS

Electroconvulsive Therapy (ECT)

The medical form of treatment with the longest history as a treatment for mental illness, other than medication, is ECT. The use of strong electric currents with minimal anesthesia producing violent convulsions and side effects like serious memory loss has given ECT a bad reputation, and it was rarely used for many years. The introduction of much better equipment, more patient-friendly techniques, more patient education, better anesthesia, and the control of a patient's convulsive responses have led to more frequent use of ECT today. It is now considered to be an effective and fast-acting treatment intervention for unipolar depression. This treatment has not produced damage visible on brain scans in humans or animals. However, there is frequently permanent memory loss for events during and immediately prior to treatment. Although ECT is proven to be an effective treatment, it is not commonly used, and in the United States only about 100,000 treatment episodes per year are recorded.

Deep Brain Stimulation

This sophisticated new treatment involves the surgical implantation of a device that will deliver an electrical current to a specific part of the brain to normalize its activity. Presently, it is only being used experimentally but has begun to show encouraging results. The FDA approved it for use in treating tremors in Parkinson's disease as well as other movement disorders. Although it has been used for other medical problems, it is only being used as an investigatory treatment for psychiatric disorders including depression; it appears to offer some promise and may prove helpful in the treatment of depression when nothing else has worked.

Rapid Transcranial Magnetic Stimulation (rTMS)

This experimental technique involves placing an electromagnetic coil on the scalp while a pulsed, high-intensity magnetic current is passed through the coil to change the way the brain functions. Since it does not produce seizures and does not require anesthesia, it seems to be a more acceptable form of treatment than ECT. The results of this treatment for depression are far too preliminary to form an opinion. However, since it appears to be safe and less invasive than some of the other medical treatments, there is hope that it might be an effective and safe treatment for depression.

Magnetic Seizure Therapy

This new approach combines ECT and rTMS as a form of treatment that induces seizures, but it has fewer side effects than ECT alone. This is a promising new technique, but is so new that it is still in development and much remains to be done to determine its effectiveness and safety.

Vagus Nerve Stimulation (VNS)

The vagus nerve is one of the cranial nerves that appears to be related to depression. VNS involves a surgical implantation of a device that stimulates the vagus nerve in a programmed sequence and at regular intervals. Supposedly, it affects the levels of some of the neurotransmitters, but little is actually known about how it works. The earliest literature suggests that it may effectively treat depression that has not previously responded to more conventional forms of treatment, and it was approved for use by the FDA in July 2005.

Light Therapy

It has been demonstrated that some people develop depression during the late fall and winter, with it getting better in the spring. This condition is known as seasonal affective disorder (SAD) and is more prevalent the farther north or south of the equator that a person lives. It is assumed that some people will show physical changes in their bodies during the darker months that will lead to depression, and the addition of more light to their environment may help with SAD.

The use of artificial light for several hours every day in the winter is called light therapy, or phototherapy. Some researchers report that this form of treatment for SAD often will reduce or even eliminate the symptoms of depression. Most professionals hesitate to recommend an expensive light box before other methods have been tried first. In fact, if one looks at all of the research, the conclusions are not quite as emphatically supportive as some would lead us to believe. In fact, there are mixed findings and unclear results that make it difficult to interpret the data and to draw conclusions from it. Some clinicians have found it is just as helpful to encourage their patients to pursue activities outside during the daylight hours such as walking. Simple little things like good nutrition, avoiding alcohol or recreational drugs, getting appropriate sleep, and even hand washing can help. Hand washing? Think about it; washing one's hands is a very good way to keep from getting sick. If you become ill during the winter months, it is very easy to slip back into habits of staying in bed, avoiding activity, and socially isolating, and for some this will usher in an episode of depression.

Exercise

It has been known for centuries that vigorous activity can help elevate someone from the depths of despair. However, we are only now beginning to understand how exercise serves as a therapeutic activity in the treatment of depression as well as other conditions. One study demonstrated that both exercise and social contact resulted in a decrease in depressive symptoms. However, only the exercise condition resulted in the decrease of the physical symptoms of depression. We now understand how important exercise is for both physical and mental health, and most mental health practitioners include regular exercise as a component of the total treatment program for their patients with depression (as well as many other conditions).

ALTERNATIVE TREATMENTS

Many people who cannot access traditional treatments—or who may prefer it—can turn to alternative forms of treatment for depression. There are many different types of alternative treatments, including manual therapies such as chiropractic, massage, and acupressure. Others may use herbs and teas, and many will use vitamins and nutritional supplements. Additional forms of alternative therapies are yoga, meditation, tai chi, traditional Chinese medicine, other Eastern medical traditions, and Native American healing rituals. Most of the proponents of these treatments are quick to point out that they are not recommending them as replacements for usual forms of treatment, but they do urge patients and mental health professionals to keep an open mind, particularly for those patients who do not respond quickly or completely to conventional treatments.

St. John's Wort

Hypericum perforatum, or St. John's Wort (SJW), has been used in Europe for many years for the treatment of depression, and it has been used more frequently in the United States in the past couple of decades. Most of the evidence collected has been anecdotal or based on minimal and inadequate research. In recent years, however, some good studies evaluating the effects of SJW show that it can be helpful in the treatment of mild to moderate depression. The conclusions on SJW are:

- It is better than placebo (a "sugar pill"), sometimes.
- It is equivalent to low doses of some of the older antidepressants (tricyclics).
- In two large studies that compare SJW to newer antidepressants like Prozac and other similar drugs, it was clear that the newer antidepressants were clearly superior.
- Basically, the side effect profile is safe, although there can be some adverse effects and some interactions with other medications.

Interestingly, many people who use SJW will do so because they think it is safer than the medications they might receive from their physician since it is natural. However, "natural" alone does not make it safe, and as the FDA does not have authority over natural supplements, the manufacturers are not held to the same standards of production and proof as are regular medications. St. John's Wort may have a place in the treatment arsenal for depression, but at this point the evidence is not very compelling.

Omega-3 Fish Oil

In recent years there has been increasing interest in the use of omega-3 oils as supplements for better health. There is evidence that these substances benefit people by decreasing risk for heart disease, high cholesterol, some types of cancer, as well as other conditions. There has also been some attention given to omega-3 fatty acids as a potential preventive agent and/or as a treatment for depression.

One line of research has looked at the consumption of fish and the incidence rates for depression. They found a highly significant relationship that strongly suggests that the more fish one eats, the less likely one is to suffer from major depression. They also reported that mothers who ate more fish were less likely to suffer from postpartum depression. Of course, this finding must be followed by the warning that for anyone, particularly prospective mothers, pregnant women, and new mothers, there is a risk for heavy metal contamination (e.g., mercury) in fish, which could be dangerous for a new baby or developing fetus and could be harmful to others as well.

However, before making major changes in one's diet, consider the risks of a high fish diet. For example, many people who are familiar with the positive effects of omega-3 oils will only eat fish once a week because of the potential for contamination. However, if you take *processed* fish oil tablets, which are contaminant free, you will also receive the benefits of omega-3 fatty acids without the fishy aftertaste. Some people add flax seed to their diets, which also has another omega-3 fatty acid, but it has not been shown to have antidepressant effects. It may, however, offer other positive health benefits.

Circadian Rhythm Treatments

There is evidence that many people with depression experience disturbances with their sleep/wake cycle and other bodily rhythms. Modifying these patterns with the hormone melatonin is a way of restoring normal sleep patterns in depressed patients with insomnia. There is some evidence that using melatonin in the afternoon, along with bright light in the morning, may help patients with SAD, but since melatonin is a hormone produced in the body, a patient should not take it without consulting their physician.

Patients for whom nothing seems to work as treatment for their depression have experimented with modifying their own sleep patterns intentionally. For example, patients who have not responded to conventional treatments may deprive themselves of partial or full episodes of sleep and feel an improvement in their general mood and functioning. This type of "treatment" may be helpful but needs to be supervised by a health professional who is experienced in dealing with depression and sleep problems.

Additional Alternative Substances

There are a variety of other nutritional supplements and vitamins that may have some effect in helping people who suffer from depression.

However, since none of them have demonstrated any positive effects that are supported in the research literature, they will not be discussed here. Suffice it to say that there are many (often well-meaning) people who may try to sell a "new" natural substance that treats depression, and "it is so new that the doctors do not even know about it yet," save your money— if there are new treatments that are effective the doctors *do* already know about them.

SUMMARY

We have a wealth of effective and safe medical treatments that are available today, and each year new and better medications that provide a different approach to managing depressive symptoms are developed. Some of the older treatments like ECT have become better and safer, and some of the new experimental approaches hold significant promise for the future. Today's drugs and medical treatment methods are so much better than those in the past—even a decade ago—that more people are being diagnosed and treated than ever before.

However, with all of the impressive advances there are some cautionary notes as well. For example, the newer antidepressant medications are so much safer and produce fewer problematic side effects that they are being used much more frequently and for a wider range of problems. This may mean that they may be used more frequently than needed; these drugs are also primarily prescribed by non–mental health professionals. The best option is for a mental health provider to prescribe medications, but sometimes the only provider available to a patient is a primary care physician or a nurse practitioner. The patient and the provider need to keep an open dialogue about treatment responses, side effects, and other concerns.

9

❖❖❖

Pulling It All Together: What Do We Know?

Depression is a common and complex mood disorder affecting many people in all cultures around the world. This condition includes biological, psychological, and social issues, and to understand and treat this disorder, all of these factors need to be considered. As pervasive, troubling, and expensive as depression is, there are a variety of effective treatments available that can help most people with depression *if* they have access to these treatments. In addition, when examining issues involving depression, there are many social and financial issues that also impact the diagnosis and treatment of depression as well.

EFFECTIVE TREATMENTS FOR DEPRESSION

According to the National Institutes of Mental Health (NIMH) more than 80 percent of people with depression will improve with appropriate treatment; that is an impressive statistic. The operative phrase is "appropriate treatment." As mentioned earlier, only about 20 of every 100 depressed persons receive appropriate treatment, and of these 20, 16 (80 percent) should be expected to improve. The treatment for a mood disorder basically has three goals:

1. Relieve symptoms
2. Restore the person's ability to function socially and in the workplace
3. Reduce the likelihood of recurrence

Likewise, there are three stages of treatment for any mood disorder:

1. Acute treatment—relieving symptoms and restoring the person to a normal level of functioning
2. Continuation treatment—stabilizing the patient and preventing relapse
3. Maintenance treatment—preventing a new episode from emerging

While these two lists seem similar, they are not the same, although the goals of treatment should link up with the stages of treatment. It is important to combine both lists when treating people suffering from mood disorders and to work toward several goals simultaneously: relieving the immediate distress, helping return the person to a state of wellness, avoiding the condition worsening, and preventing future episodes if possible.

Medication is the most common form of treatment for depression, and results suggest that an antidepressant medication can help 70 percent of depressed patients. Psychotherapy works as well as medication but may take longer to produce results; however, the effects of psychotherapy will last longer than the effects of medication. Typically, the most severe cases of depression are best treated initially with medication, but some studies have shown that the combination of medication and psychotherapy is more effective than either treatment modality alone. However, there are also some more recent studies that demonstrate that psychotherapy alone is at least as effective as medication plus psychotherapy and that given the amount of time it takes for antidepressants to take effect, medication is not that much quicker to work. Research and clinical practice indicate that psychotherapy alone or psychotherapy plus medication are the most accepted forms of treatment. *There is no credible research indicating that medication alone is the best form of treatment.*

Although psychotherapy seems to be more effective and longer lasting than medication, physicians still prescribe medication as the primary form of treatment for depression. The use of antidepressant medications has increased substantially in the last several decades and continues to increase. In fact, more prescriptions were written for antidepressant medications than for drugs treating high blood pressure, high cholesterol, asthma, or headaches. Evidence strongly supports that the use of antidepressant medication has significantly increased with the introduction of the second-generation antidepressants. Keep in mind that antidepressants are prescribed for other conditions as well, including anxiety disorders, pain disorders, peripheral neuropathy, migraine, fibromyalgia, and others.

Why does the trend of increased prescribing of antidepressants continue when compelling evidence demonstrates the importance of nonpharmacologic treatment methods? First, powerful advertising campaigns from drug companies plant the idea that their medication is the *only* type of treatment that really works. Second, it is cheaper for insurance and managed care companies to have doctors prescribe medication than to pay for several sessions of psychotherapy, and their policies and practices reflect that bias. However, most evidence supports the idea that psychotherapy is cheaper in the long term for the insurance companies by reducing relapse rates, but their policies do not suggest that they are aware of this fact.

There are also disadvantages to taking medication as a treatment for depression, the most obvious being side effects. There is no medication that is totally without side effects, including antidepressants. Although the newer drugs typically have fewer side effects, they can still be problematic, and this is the main reason most people discontinue them. Also, for medication to be effective it requires strict adherence to a medication regimen, plus visits to the physician to monitor progress. Finally, there is no antidepressant medication that works quickly; all of them take weeks or even months to reach therapeutic efficacy. Another problem is that while psychotherapy is better than medication at preventing recurrence, people receiving medication as the sole treatment may be protected from a recurrence if they *never* come off of the medication and as long as the medication continues to be effective. While most antidepressant medications appear to be safe over time, it is still prudent to take medication only when you need to; if there are effective treatments that don't require medication, then they ought to be considered.

Although patients receiving psychotherapy can relapse into a depression, the relapse rate is still less than for patients taking medication alone. However, the longer a person is in psychotherapeutic or medication treatment, the less likely they are to relapse. Thus, to effectively treat depression, treatment must begin as early as possible and continue beyond the point at which there is symptomatic relief; this is true for both medication and psychotherapy.

Improved research on effective treatments indicates that, in general, cognitive, interpersonal, and biological therapies are all effective treatments for mild to severe unipolar depression. Even more impressive is the range of other psychological and biological therapies that appear to be very helpful even when not used as a first line treatment. We must move past the notion that the only way to treat depression is with drugs.

MAKING TREATMENTS MORE EFFECTIVE

There are some factors regarding the use of medication, psychotherapy, and other forms of treatment that can be modified and "fine-tuned" to make them more responsive to individual patient needs. Making sure that the treatment plan fits the needs, preferences, and personality of the patient is essential. Making treatments more effective is important to ensure that adequate and appropriate psychological and medical therapies are available to all of the people who need them. Focusing more on underserved communities is necessary to improve the effectiveness of treatment in general, as only about 20 percent of people who report depression have received any type of counseling or psychotherapy in the past year; this rate is even lower in the minority communities. African Americans, Hispanics, Asians, Native Americans, Alaskan Natives, the elderly, and the poor are especially lacking in adequate treatment and tend to either discontinue or be dropped from treatment prematurely. Since the disease burden of depression on families and on society is significant, especially for those who are on public assistance or disability, providing effective treatment to those who suffer from depression will help to relieve some of this burden.

One area of concern is the number of people who are caregivers and who suffer from untreated depression. Better in-home care of the elderly and those with chronic illnesses has extended life spans and replaced the need for institutional care for many. The increased burden on those who must fulfill the care-giving responsibilities can lead to symptoms of depression and, unfortunately, this is a group of people who often neglect or ignore their own personal, psychological, and medical needs. Primary care physicians (PCPs) can overlook symptoms of depression in caregivers because the situation provides an easily accepted explanation for their feelings. The caregivers themselves ignore their own needs and must be frequently reminded that they will be less able to care for their loved one or friend if they become ill themselves.

Another group of people who will often suffer from depression are those with chronic impairments from illness, accidents, or other forms of disability. Unfortunately, symptoms are often ignored or explained away without treatment. Regardless of the source, depression can and should be treated at the earliest opportunity in order to lessen symptoms as well as the chance of complications (e.g., recurrence). People who suffer from long-term impairments show considerable benefits from treatment for depression, whether depression is a primary or secondary condition, and it is often a complicating factor for other medical conditions.

Another issue that complicates a patient's ability to receive treatment is the site of service—where is the treatment provided? The primary care office is the most common site for the treatment of depression, which carries with it both advantages and disadvantages. The three primary reasons for antidepressant medications failing are (1) they are not used at high enough doses, (2) they are discontinued too soon, or (3) they are continued for many years unchecked or unchanged. A PCP may not be adequately familiar with psychiatric drugs to feel comfortable with being aggressive with dosages and may not be willing to try to "push through" the side effect problems to see if they will decrease or disappear. Further, the PCP may not know enough about a specific drug to counsel the patient that taking it for a longer period of time is needed in order to give the medication the necessary time to become effective. These types of situations can often lead the PCP to discontinue or change medications too quickly. If a patient doesn't say anything about their medication and the PCP is focused on a different presenting problem, the side effects or the lack of progress from the drug might not even be discussed. If the PCP doesn't ask, the patient will often keep silent.

The PCP, however, has a significant advantage in knowing the patient and their health history and is in an excellent position to know what the patient may need, but he or she may not have all the treatment options to offer. Education in the new psychotropic medications is sometimes limited to the information presented by the drug representatives who bring lunch to the office in exchange for an opportunity to demonstrate the drug (or drugs) their company is offering. Since it is sometimes difficult to make an appointment with a psychiatrist who has a full calendar or if the patient lives in a remote area, the PCP appears to be the only opportunity for care regarding depression. Finally, PCPs can feel pressured to choose the least expensive treatment for some of their patients, which may mean prescribing the least expensive medications instead of referring their patients for treatment to a mental health provider who may be more knowledgeable. This pressure for cost containment may come from insurance or managed care companies or even from the patient who perhaps cannot afford multiple copayments, but these pressures may sometimes dictate treatment decisions and may, unfortunately, result in less effective treatment options.

OTHER WAYS TO IMPROVE THE TREATMENTS FOR DEPRESSION AND OTHER MOOD DISORDERS

The standard treatments for depression are usually different from those used to treat bipolar disorder (BPD). Although psychotherapy is usually a "primary" form of treatment for depression, it is not typically the first line of treatment for BPD. Since the primary treatment for BPD is usually medication, other forms of treatment such as "talk therapy" are sometimes underutilized. However, researchers point out that in patients with bipolar depression, the use of intensive psychotherapy in addition to psychiatric medications significantly improves treatment results. In the past, people with BPD were not usually offered psychotherapy. We now know that during manic episodes patients are too disorganized and too impulsive to benefit from psychotherapy, and that patients experiencing hypomania often feel so good they don't want to change. Therefore, when offering psychotherapy to bipolar patients we are typically referring only to depressed bipolar patients between manic or hypomanic episodes. However, there is ample evidence that psychotherapy can provide many advantages for the bipolar patient. For example, as with most mood disorders, comorbid conditions may not respond to medication for BPD but may be treatable with appropriate psychotherapy. Further, if patients can learn to recognize and cope with symptoms during the early onset of an episode, then aggressive treatment may lessen the impact of the episode both on the patient and the family. Finally, and most importantly, psychotherapy can help patients and their families learn how to cope with a chronic and recurring condition. Most people with BPD will experience approximately three episodes every decade, so it is important that they learn how to recognize and deal with them when they occur.

TREATING POSTPARTUM DEPRESSION

Although frequently ignored and misunderstood, this unfortunately common form of depression is quite treatable in most circumstances. There are several types of postpartum mood disorders that include what is often called the "baby blues," which is very common and is not an "official" diagnosis. This may last from a few hours to a few days but typically goes away within two weeks. Reassurance and emphasizing the importance of adequate sleep/rest is usually appropriate treatment. A mild medication may be used for insomnia, but if the mother is nursing this should be considered carefully. The main concern is to monitor the mother to make sure that the depression does not worsen.

A rare and more serious form of postpartum mood disorder is postpartum psychosis (PPP) and is often found in those who have experienced serious psychological conditions such as schizophrenia or bipolar disorder prior to pregnancy. Fortunately, if women who suffer from these conditions are on appropriate medication and are monitored closely, they can experience pregnancy and delivery with few problems. However, when a mother experiences PPP she must take medication and may need to be hospitalized. Electroconvulsive therapy has also proven to be an effective treatment for PPP and for more severe forms of postpartum mood disorder.

Postpartum depression (PPD) can be treated effectively if it is detected, but, unfortunately, many mothers do not report how badly they feel or perhaps their physicians are so focused on the health of the baby or the physical recovery of the mother that they might not notice a psychological problem. Some mothers may feel guilty because they do not feel as happy as was expected; feel self-conscious, embarrassed, or afraid; or they may not know how to identify or explain what they are feeling. Providing appropriate mental health treatment for mothers suffering from PPD is a problem in every country where we have data and research. While this situation is improving in North America and Europe compared to other parts of the world, it remains an issue of concern everywhere.

If PPD is not treated appropriately the depression is more likely to continue longer and may become a more complex and difficult problem. Also, inadequate treatment of PPD increases immediate and future risks to the mother and to the child. As with many other conditions, early detection and treatment of PPD leads to a more favorable treatment result. Although the cause of PPD is somewhat unique, there is no reason to believe that it needs to be treated differently from any other form of depression. The main treatments for PPD include medication, psychotherapy, or both. For mothers who are breast-feeding or want to avoid medication and are experiencing mild to moderate PPD, good results have been reported from using cognitive-behavioral psychotherapy, interpersonal psychotherapy, group psycho-educational therapy, and support groups. In terms of medication, exactly the same approach is used with mothers suffering from PPD as other forms of depression. Typically, the second-generation drugs are tried first and then others depending upon the side effect profile and the specific symptoms.

It has also been established that psychosocial treatment for prospective mothers can produce a protective effect prior to delivery, thus reducing the frequency of PPD. When prospective mothers are provided with appropriate support and information, they are less likely to have difficulties like PPD following the birth of their child. The mother also needs support following the birth so that she does not take out her frustrations on the baby and can use more positive and effective parenting techniques. She also needs to take care of herself and her own needs, which is frequently difficult while trying to manage the new life she is responsible for. In addition, bonding with and establishing a nurturing relationship with the baby is important for the mother and for the child. For new mothers to take care of themselves also requires help from their spouse, partner, family, and friends—without this help they cannot do a very good job of meeting their own needs as well as those of their baby.

WHAT PATIENTS CAN DO TO DEAL WITH DEPRESSION

One of the worst things about being depressed is feeling so miserable that you can't stand it, and being so immobilized by the disorder that you can't do anything about it. When people are depressed or can feel they are becoming depressed, they often don't have any idea as to what they can do to improve the situation or who to turn to for help. Unfortunately, there are many things that people will reach for first that only make the situation worse. Turning to recreational drugs and/or alcohol, socially isolating, eating too much (or too little), spending too much money, and getting involved in activities that will cause difficulties (e.g., gambling) are examples of what will only make a difficult situation even worse. So what *should* people do? Although the depressed patient will find reasons why any suggestion is either wrong or won't work, it is important that the depressed patient do something—anything positive that has a chance to help. Talking to their primary care physician (PCP) is a good place to start. The PCP may recommend medication, but they will also be able to refer a patient to a psychologist, psychiatrist, or other mental health professional; perhaps the patient had prior contact with a mental health professional or knows someone who has. Patients can contact their health maintenance organization or a managed care plan through their health insurance program to seek a recommendation of mental health professionals in their plan; they are usually listed by zip code. Community mental health clinics, hospitals with mental health or psychiatric clinics, and clinics at a university or medical school may offer outpatient services to the public; state mental hospitals often provide outpatient clinics as well. If a person is feeling very distraught or suicidal, the local emergency room is the best place to go. Some hospitals have a psychiatric unit where people can receive inpatient care on a short-term basis. Most communities have family service agencies, social service agencies, church-sponsored counseling centers, or private clinics and facilities that provide services. If a person doesn't know where to turn for help, then a clergy person is someone who usually knows where to refer someone. Places of employment may also be a good reference source—many companies offer employee assistance programs that can provide brief counseling or can refer a person to clinics or to another professional. Finally, a person can look online or in the yellow pages of the phone book and call a local medical or psychological society for a referral to a licensed professional. It is important that the chosen professional is licensed to provide mental health services, which means that they have met the educational and professional standards in their field that qualifies them to offer these services.

In addition to reaching out for professional help, there are several things that people suffering from depression can do to help themselves. Depressed people have difficulty with motivating themselves to do anything, but if they sit around waiting for motivation to occur they may be waiting for a long time. It is important to move and do something; set short-term, reasonable goals and hold yourself accountable for fulfilling them, but don't blame others, the weather, etc. for not completing your goals—just do it.

When people are depressed the small tasks in life seem so huge that they tend to be put on hold, become bigger, and multiply. Break large tasks into smaller ones and set priorities. Don't try to do too many things at once and take short breaks. Making even a little progress is better than not doing anything at all. Don't avoid people; find someone close to you whom you can confide in. Stay active doing things you like to do. This may be difficult because you may not feel good at the time, but the activities will have a cumulative effect, and the more you do the sooner you will begin to feel "normal" again. Get involved with mild exercise and some recreational and social events. If you don't feel like doing much, then do just a little; but do something. Don't look for quick fixes or rapid solutions—getting better takes time and persistence. People don't "snap out" of depression, but rather they gradually start to see progress and then begin to feel better. Frequently, people suffering from depression want to *be* better, but they often don't want to do the work to *get* better.

It is important for people suffering from depression to realize that when depressed you do not think about things as you normally would and, therefore, it is best if you don't try to make major decisions unless you absolutely need to; seek advice from people you trust. Although positive thinking is challenging while a person is depressed, it can start to produce some small changes in the way you think and feel. One piece of advice that is difficult for the depressed to accept is to "let people help you." Depressed people feel helpless and hopeless and most feel like a burden to everyone else. It is difficult to ask for help, but this one step may be the single thing that actually spurs improvement.

Another idea that can often help with depression is caring for a pet such as a cat, dog, bird, or even fish or hermit crabs. Pets are a significant boon to mental health and can certainly help people with depression. Having a pet can facilitate social interaction and exercise by taking the pet for a walk and seeing friends and neighbors, but the pet can be a source of a meaningful relationship itself. The responsibility of caring for a pet can also provide a much needed and important activity. If keeping a pet is not realistic, it may be possible to borrow or care for the pets of others as a way to enjoy a pet with minimal commitment, inconvenience, or expense, while helping someone else at the same time.

Considering the things that people can do to help those with depression, it is important to remember that the best form of treatment for any condition is *prevention*, and this is especially true of depression. Taking care of our physical and emotional health is a responsibility that cannot be taken too lightly and, yet, most of us neglect to do the most basic things to care for ourselves. Smoking, drinking alcohol, using recreational drugs, overeating, eating poorly, not seeking medical or psychological help when needed, and not exercising are all things that we have control over. To not exert that control is asking for trouble; it is important that we stay physically and socially active.

PROBLEMS IN RECEIVING ADEQUATE TREATMENT FOR DEPRESSION

With rising health care costs and managed care companies controlling access to care, it is becoming more difficult to obtain appropriate mental health care for an adequate period of time. In fact, the current climate for mental health care has overturned more than a century of clinical wisdom and experience that has demonstrated that, given appropriate care in a timely fashion for an adequate length of time, the large majority of people with depression improve. Presently, for example, it is often difficult to get a suicidal patient admitted into the hospital, and it is even more difficult to keep them hospitalized long enough to be clinically stabilized or to receive adequate treatment. This makes most acute conditions challenging to treat if they are severe enough to warrant hospitalization, and even when hospitalized, patients are often not allowed to stay long enough to get appropriate treatment started and then continued out of the hospital—often it seems like the main goal for hospitalized patients is just to get the them discharged as soon as possible.

Inadequate access to care is a primary constraint in the development of a reasonable national mental health system. Presently, our system is primarily crisis-oriented and many conditions are not treated appropriately. The current mental health treatment system in the United States is an international embarrassment, so woefully inadequate that there is no justification for how bad it has become.

One of the true tragedies in American health care is that we in many ways have the best available health and mental health care in the world, but in terms of delivering services to those who need them, we are behind the times. According to the statistics regarding the quality of health care delivery systems, the United States does not even rank in the top 20; in fact, according to the World Health Organization the United States is ranked 37th in the world in terms of the quality of health care.

SUMMARY

The picture is clear:

- Depression is a serious and common problem that affects people of all social and racial groups throughout the world.
- Good and affordable treatment is available.
- With appropriate care most people with depression will get better.
- Most who have depression do not receive adequate treatment.
- We must do more and do it better.

It is not easy to tackle a problem of this magnitude, but by being responsible and taking care of our own health and mental health needs, we can reach out to help others who are dealing with depression or other mental health issues by sharing information and pointing them in the direction to find the help they need. Staying informed and becoming involved politically and socially will help to focus attention on these issues.

There are no "solutions" to the problem of depression—it will always exist in one form or another. However, by taking care of our own psychological needs and encouraging those we care about to do the same, we can make a dent. Being a good role model is important, but we should also be willing to advocate for mental health care needs with health providers, insurance companies, clinics, schools, and even politicians.

References

CHAPTER 1

Abramson, L. Y., M. E. Seligman, and J. D. Teasdale. 1978. "Learned Helplessness in Humans: Critique and Reformulation." *Journal of Abnormal Psychology* 87(1): 49–74.

American Psychiatric Association. 1998. *Let's Talk Facts about Depression.* Washington, DC: Author.

American Psychiatric Association. 2000. *Diagnostic and Statistical Manual—IV, Text Revision.* Washington, DC: Author.

Beck, A. T. 1986. "Hopelessness as a Predictor of Eventual Suicide." In *Psychobiology of Suicidal Behavior*, edited by J. J. Mann & M. Stanley, 90–96. New York: Academy of Sciences.

Druss, B. G., R. A. Rosenheck, and W. H. Sledge. 2000. "Health and Disability Costs of Depressive Illness in a Major U.S. Corporation." *American Journal of Psychiatry* 157(8): 1274–78.

Ebmeier, K. P., C. Donaghey, C. and J. D. Steele. 2006. "Recent Developments and Current Controversies in Depression." *Lancet* 367: 153–67.

McIntosh, J. L. 1991. "Epidemiology of Suicide in the U.S." In *Lifespan Perspectives of Suicide*, edited by A. A. Leenaars. New York: Plenum Press.

Nydegger, R. V. 2014. *Suicide and Mental Health.* Santa Barbara, CA: Greenwood.

Penning, B. W., S. W. Geerlings, D. J. Deeg, J. T. van Eijk, W. van Tilburg, and A. T. Beekman. 1999. "Minor and Major Depression and the Risk of Death in Older Persons." *Archives of General Psychiatry* 56(10): 889–95.

Shneidman, E. S. 2001. *Comprehending Suicide: Landmarks in 20th Century Suicidology*. Washington, DC: American Psychological Association.

Solomon, A. 2001. *The Noonday Demon: An Atlas of Depression*. New York: Scribner.

Swartz, K. L. 2007. *Depression and Anxiety White Paper*. Johns Hopkins Medicine. Bethel, CT: Medletter Associates.

CHAPTER 2

Beck, A. 2002. "Cognitive Models of Depression." In *Clinical Advances in Cognitive Psychotherapy: Theory and Application*, edited by R. L. Leahy and E. T. Dowds, 29–61. New York: Springer.

Blazer, D. G., R. C. Kessler, K. A. McGonagle, and M. S. Swartz. 1994. "The Prevalence and Distribution of Major Depression in a National Community Sample: The National Comorbidity Survey." *American Journal of Psychiatry* 151: 979–86.

Callahan, C. M., S. L. Hui, N. A. Neinaber, B. S. Musick, and W. M. Tierny. 1994. "Longitudinal Study of Depression and Health Services Use among Elderly Primary Care Patients." *Journal of the American Geriatrics Society* 42: 833–38.

Lerman, G. L., and M. Weissman. 1989. "Increasing Rates of Depression." *Journal of the American Medical Association* 261: 2229–35.

Lewinsohn, P. M., G. N. Clarke, H. Hops, and J. Andrews. 1990. "Cognitive-Behavioral Treatment for Depressed Adolescents." *Behavioral Therapy* 21: 385–401.

Monroe, S. M., and K. Hadjiyannakis. 2002. "The Social Environment and Depression: Focusing Severe Life Stress." In *Handbook of Depression: Research and Treatment*, edited by I. H. Gotlib and C. L. Hammen, 314–40. New York: Guilford.

Ohayon, M. M. 2007. "Epidemiology of Depression and Its Treatment in the General Population." *Journal of Psychiatric Research* 41(3–4): 207–213.

Power, M., ed. 2004. *Mood Disorders: A Handbook of Science and Practice*. Chichester, UK: John Wiley.

Reinherz, H. Z., R. M. Giaconia, B. Pakiz, A. B. Siverman, A. K. Frost, and E. S. Lefkowitz. 1993. "Psychosocial Risks for Major Depression in

Late Adolescence: A Longitudinal Community Study." *Journal of the American Academy of Child and Adolescent Psychiatry*, 32(6): 1155–63.

Seligman, M. E. P. 1975. *Helplessness*. San Francisco: Freeman.

Stompe, T., G. Ortwein-Swoboda, H. R. Chaudhry, A. Friedmann, T. Wenzel, and H. Schanda. 2001. "Guilt and Depression: A Cross-cultural Comparative Study." *Psychopathology* 34(6): 289–98.

Swartz, K. L. 2007. *Depression and Anxiety White Paper*. Johns Hopkins Medicine. Bethel, CT: Medletter Associates.

Thase, M. E., R. Jindal, and R. H. Howland. 2002. "Biological Aspects of Depression." In *Handbook of Depression: Research and Treatment*, edited by I. H. Gotlib and C. L. Hammen, 192–218. New York: Guilford.

CHAPTER 3

Fava, M., and K. Kendler. 2000. "Major Depressive Disorder." *Neuron* 28(2): 335–41.

Fava, M., M. A. Rankin, E. C. Wright, J. E. Alpert, A. A. Niernberg, J. Fava, and J. F. Rosenbaum. 2000. "Anxiety Disorders in Major Depression." *Comprehensive Psychiatry* 41(2): 97–102.

First, M. B., and A. Tasman, eds. 2004. *DSM-IV-TR*™ *Mental Disorders: Diagnosis, Etiology, and Treatment*. Chichester, UK: John Wiley & Sons.

Jamison, K. R. 1995. "Manic-Depressive Illness and Creativity." *Scientific American* (February): 63–67.

Katon, W. 1996. "The Impact of Major Depression on Chronic Medical Illness." *General Hospital Psychiatry* 18: 215–19.

Kemp, B. J., and L. Mosqueda, eds. 2004. *Aging with a Disability: What the Clinician Needs to Know*. Baltimore, MD: Johns Hopkins University Press.

Mueller, T. I., and A. C. Leon. 1996. "Recovery, Chronicity, and Levels of Psychopathology in Major Depression." *Psychiatric Clinics of North America* 19(1): 85–102.

Nydegger, R. 2006. "Postpartum Depression: More Than the 'Baby Blues?'" In *Mental Disorders of the New Millennium*, vol. 3, edited by T. G. Plante. Westport, CT: Praeger.

Power, M., ed. 2004. *Mood Disorders: A Handbook of Science and Practice*. Chichester, UK: John Wiley and Sons.

Regier, D. A., D. S. Rae, W. E. Narrow, C. T. Kaelber, and A. F. Schatzberg. 1998. "Prevalence of Anxiety Disorders and Their Co-morbidity with Mood and Addictive Disorders." *British Journal of Psychiatry* 173 (Suppl. 34): 24–28.

Rosenthal, N. E., and M. C. Blehar, eds. 1989. *Seasonal Affective Disorders and Phototherapy.* New York: Guilford.

Schoevers, R. A., A. T. F. Beekman, W. van Tilburg, D. J. H. Deeg, C. Joncker, M. I. Geerlings, and B. W. J. H. Penninx. 2000. "Association of Depression and Gender with Mortality in Old Age." *British Journal of Psychiatry* 117: 336–42.

Swartz, K. 2007. *Depression and Anxiety. The Johns Hopkins White Papers.* Baltimore, MD: Johns Hopkins Medicine.

Torrey, E. F., and M. B. Knable. 2002. *Surviving Manic Depression: A Manual on Bipolar Disorder for Patients, Families, and Providers.* New York: Basic Books.

CHAPTER 4

Abramson, L. Y., M. E. Seligman, and J. D. Teasdale. 1978. "Learned Helplessness in Humans: Critique and Reformulation." *Journal of Abnormal Psychology* 87(1): 49–74.

Culbertson, F. M. 1997. "Depression and Gender: An International Review." *American Psychologist* 52(1): 25–31.

Leunes, A. D., J. R. Nation, and N. M. Turley. 1980. "Male-Female Performance in Learned Helplessness." *Journal of Psychology* 104: 255–58.

McGrath, E., G. P. Keita, B. Strickland, and N. F. Russo. 1990. *Women and Depression: Risk Factors and Treatment Issues.* Washington, DC: American Psychological Association.

Nazroo, J. V. 2001. "Exploring Gender Differences in Depression." *Psychiatric Times* 17(3): 1–4.

Nolen-Hoeksema, S. 2002. "Gender Differences in Depression." In *Handbook of Depression: Research and Treatment,* edited by I. H. Gottlib and C. L. Hammen, 492–509. New York: Guilford.

Nolen-Hoeksema, S., and J. S. Girgus. 1994. "The Emergence of Gender Differences in Depression during Adolescence." *Psychological Bulletin* 115, 424–43.

Nydegger, R. 2006. "Postpartum Depression: More Than the 'Baby Blues?'" In *Mental Disorders of the New Millennium,* vol. 3, edited by T. G. Plante. Westport, CT: Praeger.

Pleck, J. 1981. *The Myth of Masculinity.* Cambridge, MA: MIT Press.

Prior, J. 1999. *Gender and Mental Health.* New York: New York University Press.

Real, T. 1997. *I Don't Want to Talk About It: Overcoming the Secret Legacy of Male Depression.* New York: Fireside.

Ryan, D., and X. Kosturas. 1995. "Psychiatric Disorders in the Postpartum Period." *BC Medical Journal* 47(2): 100–103.

Spangler, D. L., A. D. Simons, S. M. Monroe, and M. E. Thase. 1996. "Gender Differences in Cognitive Diathesis-Stress Domain Match Implications for Differential Pathways to Depression." *Journal of Abnormal Psychology* 105(4): 653–57.

Stowe, Z. N., and C. B. Nemeroff. 1995. "Women at Risk for Postpartum Onset of Major Depression." *American Journal of Obstetrics and Gynecology* 173: 639–45.

Torrey, E. F., and M. B. Knable. 2002. *Surviving Manic Depression: A Manual on Bipolar Disorder for Patients, Families, and Providers.* New York: Basic Books.

CHAPTER 5

Conwell, Y., J. M. Lyness, P. Duberstein, C. Cox, L. Seidlitz, A. DiGiorgio, and E. D. Caine. 2000. "Completed Suicide among Older Patients in Primary Care Practices: A Controlled Study." *Journal of American Geriatrics Society* 48(1): 23–29.

Downey, G., and J. C. Coyne. 1990. "Children of Depressed Parents: An Integrative Review." *Psychological Bulletin* 108: 50–76.

Hazell, P. 2005. "Depression in Children and Adolescents." *Clinical Evidence* 14: 1–16.

Kessler, R. C., S. Avenevoli, and R. Merikangus. 2001. "Mood Disorders in Children and Adolescents: An Epidemiologic Perspective." *Biological Psychiatry* 49: 1002–14.

Lam, D. H., C. R. Brewin, R. T. Woods, and P. E. Bebbington. 1987. "Cognition and Social Adversity in the Depressed Elderly." *Journal of Abnormal Psychology* 96(1): 23–26.

Reinherz, H. Z., R. M. Giaconia, A. M. C. Hauf, M. S. Wasserman, and A. B. Silverman. 1999. "Major Depression in the Transition to Adulthood: Risks and Impairments." *Journal of Abnormal Psychology* 108(3): 500–510.

Reynolds, C. F., III, M. A. Dew, B. G. Pollock, B. H. Mulsant, E. Frank, M. D. Miller, P. R. Houck, S. Mazumdar, M. A. Butters, J. A. Stack, M. H. Schlernitzaur, E. M. Whyte, A. Gildengers, J. Karp, E. Lenze, K. Szanto, S. Bensasi, and D. J. Kupfer. 2006. "Maintenance Treatment of Major Depression in Old Age." *New England Journal of Medicine* 354: 1130–38.

Ryan, N. D., J. Puig-Atich, H. Abrosini, H. Rabinovich, D. Robinson, B. Nelson, S. Tyengar, and J. Twomey. 1987. "The Clinical Pattern of

Major Depression in Children and Adolescents." *Archives of General Psychiatry* 44(10): 854–61.

Stewart, S. M., B. D. Kennard, P. W. H. Lee, C. W. Hughes, T. Mayes, G. J. Emslie, and P. M. Lewinsohn. 2004. "A Cross-cultural Investigation of Cognitions and Depressive Symptoms in Adolescents." *Journal of Abnormal Psychology* 113: 248–57.

Swartz, K. L. 2007. *Depression and Anxiety White Paper*. Johns Hopkins Medicine. Bethel, CT: Medletter Associates.

Teachman, B. A. 2006. "Aging and Negative Affect: The Rise and Fall and Rise of Anxiety and Depression Symptoms." *Psychology and Aging* 21(1): 201–7.

Williamson, G. M., and R. Schulz. 1992. "Physical Illness and Symptoms of Depression among Elderly Outpatients." *Psychology and Aging* 7(3): 343–51.

World Health Organization. 2000. *Women's Mental Health: An Evidence-Based Review*. WHO/MSD/MHP00.1. Geneva: World Health Organization.

CHAPTER 6

Beaudet, M. P. 1996. "Depression." *Health Reports* 7, 11–15.

Bell, A., and M. Weinberg. 1978. *Homosexualities: A Study of Diversity among Men and Women*. New York: Simon & Shuster.

Cheung, F. K., and L. R. Snowden. 1990. "Community Mental Health and Ethnic Minority Population." *Community Mental Health Journal* 26: 89–102.

Chin, J. L. 1998. "Mental Health Services and Treatment." In *Handbook of Asian American Psychology*, edited by L. C. Lee and N. W. S. Zane, 485–504. Thousand Oaks, CA: Sage.

Cochran, S. D., J. G. Sullivan, and V. M. Mays. 2003. "Prevalence of Mental Disorders, Psychological Distress, and Mental Health Services Use among Lesbian, Gay, and Bisexual Adults in the United States." *Journal of Consulting and Clinical Psychology* 71(1): 53–61.

Fouad, N. A., and P. Arredondo. 2007. *Becoming Culturally Oriented: Practical Advice for Psychologists and Educators*. Washington, DC: American Psychological Association.

Greene, B. 2007. "Delivering Ethical Psychological Services to Lesbian, Gay, and Bisexual Clients." In *Handbook of Counseling and Psychotherapy with Lesbian, Gay, Bisexual, and Transgender Clients*, 2nd ed. Washington, DC: American Psychological Association.

Jay, K., and A. Young. 1977. *The Gay Report: Lesbians and Gay Men Speak Out about Their Sexual Experiences and Lifestyles.* New York: Summit.

Mansfield, A. K., M. E. Addis, and W. Courtenay. 2005. "Measurement of Men's Help Seeking: Development and Evaluation of the Barriers to Help Seeking Scale." *Psychology of Men & Masculinity* 6(2): 95–108.

Matthews, C. 2007. "Affirmative Lesbian, Gay, and Bisexual Counseling with All Clients." In *Handbook of Counseling and Psychotherapy with Lesbian, Gay, Bisexual, and Transgender Clients,* 2nd ed. Washington, DC: American Psychological Association.

Moradi, B., and C. Risco. 2006. "Perceived Discrimination Experiences and Mental Health of Latina/o American Persons." *Journal of Counseling Psychology* 53(4): 411–21.

Young, A. S., R. Klap, C. D. Sherbourne, and K. B. Wells. 2001. "The Quality of Care for Depressive and Anxiety Disorders in the United States." *Archives of General Psychiatry* 58: 55–61.

CHAPTER 7

American Psychological Association. 1993. *Practice Guideline for Major Depressive Disorder in Adults.* Washington, DC: Author.

Beck, A. 2002. "Cognitive Models of Depression." In *Clinical Advances in Cognitive Psychotherapy: Theory and Application,* edited by R. L. Leahy and E. T. Dowds, 29–61. New York: Springer.

DeRubeis, R. J., S. D. Hollon, J. D. Amsterdam, R. C. Shelton, P. R. Young, R. M. Salomon, J. P. O'Reardon, M. L. Lovett, M. M. Gladis, L. L. Brown, and R. Gallop. 2001. "Cognitive Therapy vs. Medications in Treatment of Moderate to Severe Depression." *Archives of General Psychiatry* 62: 397–408.

Hopko, D. R., C. W. Lejuez, K. J. Ruggiero, and G. H. Eifert. 2003. "Contemporary Behavioral Activation Treatments for Depression: Procedures, Principles, and Progress." *Clinical Psychology Review* 23: 699–717.

Jacobson, N. S., K. S. Dobson, P. A. Truax, M. E. Addis, K. Koerner, J. K. Gollan, E. Gortner, and S. E. Prince. 1996. "A Component Analysis of Cognitive-Behavioral Treatment for Depression." *Journal of Consulting and Clinical Psychology* 64: 295–304.

Leichseuring, F. 2001. "Comparative Effects of Short-Term Psychodynamic Psychotherapy and Cognitive-Behavioral Therapy in Depression: A Meta-analytic Approach." *Clinical Psychology Review* 21(3): 401–19.

Lejuez, C. W., D. R. Hopko, and S. D. Hopko. 2001. "A Brief Behavioral Activation Treatment for Depression: Treatment Manual." *Behavior Modification* 25: 255–86.

Lewinsohn, P. M., J. M. Sullivan, and S. J. Grosscup. 1980. "Changing Reinforcing Events: An Approach to the Treatment of Depression." *Psychotherapy: Theory, Research and Practice* 47: 322–34.

Otto, M. W., J. A. Pava, and S. Sprich-Buckminster. 1996. "Treatment of Major Depression: Application and Efficacy of Cognitive-Behavioral Therapy." In *Challenges in Clinical Practice: Pharmacologic and Psychosocial Strategies*, edited by M. H. Pollack and M. W. Otto, 31–52. New York: Guilford.

Rehm, L. P. 1995. "Psychotherapies for Depression." In *Anxiety and Depression in Adults and Children*, edited by K. D. Craig and K. S. Dobson, 183–208. Thousand Oaks, CA: Sage.

Weissman, M. M., J. C. Markowitz, and G. L. Klerman. 2000. *Comprehensive Guide to Interpersonal Psychotherapy*. New York: Basic Books.

CHAPTER 8

American Psychological Association. 1993. *Practice Guideline for Major Depressive Disorder in Adults*. Washington, DC: Author.

Berman, A. L., D. A. Jobes, and M. M. Silverman. 2006. *Adolescent Suicide: Assessment and Intervention*, 2nd ed. Washington, DC: American Psychological Association.

Dukakis, K., and L. Tye. 2006. *Shock: The Healing Power of Electroconvulsive Therapy*. New York: Penguin.

Ebmeier, K. P., A. Berge, D. Semple, P. Shah, and D. Steele. 2004. "Biological Treatments in Mood Disorders." In Mood Disorders: A Handbook of Science and Practice, edited by Mick Power, 143–66. Chichester, UK: John Wiley and Sons.

Gitlin, M. J., R. Suri, L. Altshuler, J. Zuckerbrow-Miller, and L. Fairbanks. 2002. "Bupropion-Sustained Release as a Treatment for SSRI-Induced Sexual Side Effects." *Sex & Marital Therapy* 28(2): 131–38.

Goldman, B. D. 1999. "The Circadian Time System and Reproduction in Mammals." *Steroids* 64(9): 679–85.

Hibbeln, J. R. 1998. "Seafood Consumption, the DHA Content of Mothers' Milk, and Prevalence Rates of Postpartum Depression: A Cross-national, Ecological Analysis." *Journal of Affective Disorders* 69: 15–29.

Linde, K., G. Ramirez, C. D. Mulrow, A. Pauls, W. Weidenhammer, and D. Melchart. 1996. "St. John's Wort for Depression—An Overview and Meta-analysis of Randomized Clinical Trials." *British Medical Journal* 313: 253–58.

McNeil, J. K., E. M. LeBlanc, and M. Joyner. 1991. "The Effect of Exercise on Depressive Symptoms in the Moderately Depressed Elderly." *Psychology and Aging* 6(3): 487–88.

Milane, M. S., M. A. Suchard, M. L. Wong, and J. Licinio. 2006. "Modeling of the Temporal Patterns of Fluoxetine Prescriptions and Suicide Rates in the United States." *Public Library of Science Medicine* 3: 816.

Power, M., ed. *Mood Disorders: A Handbook of Science and Practice.* Chichester, UK: John Wiley and Sons.

Rosenthal, N. E., and M. C. Blehar, eds. 1989. *Seasonal Affective Disorder & Phototherapy.* New York: Guilford.

Sandler, M. 1990. "Monoamine Oxidase Inhibitors in Depression: History and Mythology." *Journal of Psychopharmacology* 4(3): 136–39.

Swartz, K. L. 2007. *Depression and Anxiety White Paper.* Johns Hopkins Medicine. Bethel, CT: Medletter Associates.

Wirz-Justice, A., and R. H. Van den Hoofdakker. 1999. "Sleep Deprivation in Depression: What Do We Know, Where Do We Go?" *Biological Psychiatry* 46(4): 445–53.

CHAPTER 9

Berman, A. L., D. A. Jobes, and M. M. Silverman. 2006. *Adolescent Suicide: Assessment and Intervention.* Washington, DC: American Psychological Association.

Bowden, C. L. 2001. "Strategies to Reduce Misdiagnosis of Bipolar Depression." *Psychiatric Services* 52(1): 51–55.

Calabrese, J. R., L. B. Marangell, L. Gyulai, M. Araga, J. M. Gonzalez, E. R. Shirley, M. E. Thase, and G. S. Sachs. 2007. "Psychosocial Treatments for Bipolar Depression." *Archives of General Psychiatry* 64: 419–27.

Kahan, J. S., J. M. Mitchell, B. J. Kemp, and R. H. Adkins. 2006. "The Results of a 6-Month Treatment for Depression on Symptoms, Life Satisfaction, and Community Activities among Individuals Aging with a Disability." *Rehabilitation Psychology* 51(1): 13–22.

Lickey, M. E., and B. Gordon. 1991. *Medicine and Mental Illness: The Use of Drugs in Psychiatry.* New York: W. H. Freeman.

Miklowitz, D. J., et al. 2007. "Intensive Psychosocial Intervention Enhances Functioning in Patients with Bipolar Depression: Results from a 9-Month Randomized Controlled Trial." *American Journal of*

Psychiatry 164(9): 1340–47. doi: http://dx.doi.org/10.1176/appi.ajp.2007.07020311

Nonacs, R., A. C. Viguera, and L. S. Cohen. 2005. "Psychiatric Aspects of Pregnancy." In *Women's Mental Health*, edited by S. G. Kornstein and A. H. Clayton, 70–90. New York: Guilford.

O'Hara, M. W., S. Scott, L. L. Gorman, and A. Wenzel. 2000. "Efficacy of Interpersonal Psychotherapy for Postpartum Depression." *Archives of General Psychiatry* 57: 1039–45.

Olfson, M., and G. L. Klerman. 1993. "Trends in the Prescription of Antidepressants by Office-Based Psychiatrists." *American Journal of Psychiatry* 150: 571–77.

Prior, J. 1999. *Gender and Mental Health*. New York: New York University Press.

Scott, J. 2007. "Bipolar Disorders." In *Handbook of Evidence-Based Psychotherapies: A Guide for Research and Practice*, edited by C. Freeman and M. Powers, 301–13. Chichester, UK: John Wiley & Sons.

Swartz, K. 2007. *Depression and Anxiety*. The Johns Hopkins White Papers. Baltimore, MD: Johns Hopkins Medicine.

Weissman, M. M., J. C. Markowitz, and G. L. Klerman. 2000. *Comprehensive Guide to Interpersonal Psychotherapy*. New York: Basic Books.

Index

About the Author

Rudy Nydegger, PhD, ABPP, is a board certified clinical psychologist and also a professor of psychology at Union College and a professor of management at the School of Management at Union Graduate College. He is presently the chair of the Division of Psychology at Ellis Hospital in Schenectady, New York. He has practiced, taught, done research, and written about psychology for over forty years and is continuing to do so today. In addition, he is the immediate past-president and chair of the Board of the National Register of Health Service Psychologists. He is also past-president of the New York State Psychological Association and the Psychological Association of Northeastern New York. Further, he is a past board member of the New York State Board of Psychology. He has written books on depression, anxiety, and suicide and is coauthor of a book on workplace violence. He has contributed many other chapters in books, sections in encyclopedias, and scholarly articles.